VENTURE OF FAITH

VENTURE OF FAITH

The Story of the Writers' Summer School

1949–1982

by

NANCY MARTIN

H. E. WALTER LTD

First published in 1983 by
H. E. Walter Ltd.
26 Grafton Road, Worthing
West Sussex BN11 1QU, England

ISBN 0 85479 066 7

Printed and bound in Great Britain at
The Camelot Press Ltd, Southampton

CONTENTS

FOREWORD

When a venture like the Writers' Summer School becomes an institution, it is fitting that an accessible record of its history should be written, and especially an account of its beginnings – we know the oak, but what was the acorn like? No one is better equipped to tell the story than Nancy Martin, the founder Secretary of the School, who might herself be described as a well-loved Swanwick institution.

Forewords are usually written by celebrities or authorities in the field in the hope of lending stature to the book and enhancing sales. I cannot think why Nancy should have wanted me to write this one. Though not particularly given to modesty, I certainly cannot claim to be a celebrity, and my knowledge of the School is limited to the experience of recent years. As for lending stature to the book, that it has already, and its sales are assured, for every member of the School, past and present, and many others too, will undoubtedly want a copy. However, when Nancy asked me to write a Foreword I could only accept the honour with great pleasure.

Everyone who has benefited from the Writers' Summer School – and there are very many – owes a great debt to those who began this "venture of faith". Now we owe even more to Nancy Martin for writing this history, which I warmly commend to all its readers.

Michael Legat

INTRODUCTION

The founding of the Writers' Summer School really was a venture of faith. There is little, if anything, in this materialistic world which can be organised without finance, a venue, secretary or treasurer and with a Chairman who has just been told by his medical adviser to give up his business and go and live in the wide open spaces. Yet, in spite of these conditions being applicable, the Writers' Summer School did take off most successfully in 1949 and soon became the firmly established event it is today, showing every sign of surviving for another thirty-four years. Ever since that first School it has been an annual event, eagerly anticipated by writers and would-be writers, many of whom return again and again, while every year about fifty applicants are too late to secure a place even six months before the School is due to commence.

As the only member of the original committee still connected with the School, and as one who has attended and been involved in it for thirty-three of its thirty-four years of existence, I have been invited to write this history. It was Stanley Wilson who first approached me about doing so and he it was who brought the matter before the committee of the 1981 School in the form of a resolution. It was agreed that this ought to be done, and I was committed. It has been an enjoyable and nostalgic task, and I wish to record my appreciation and thanks to all those members who have sent me their recollections and experiences, from which I have freely quoted. I should have liked to include many, many more extracts from the letters I have received, but alas, space did not permit. My thanks and apologies, then, to those whose words do not appear in the book. I also wish to acknowledge my indebtedness to Messrs. Hutchinson for allowing me to quote from their reports in *The Writer*, and especially to Victor Allan for the pieces I have reprinted from his excellent prize-winning article on that first Summer School.

The first three Schools, in 1949, 50 and 51, were known as the Writers Circles' Summer School, with Circle members being given priority of place. Since then it has become known as the Writers' Summer School. In 1949 the London Writer Circle was represented by 47 members, while 25 members of Croydon Writers' Circle attended. A letter from the Birmingham Writers' Group sums up the effect of that first event in the following terms: "It was the unanimous opinion of the committee last Wednesday evening that I should write you on behalf of the Birmingham members who attended the Summer School and record our conviction that the School was a resounding success from beginning to end. We realise our indebtedness to you for the hours of work you put in as Secretary and to the organising committee for their enterprise and faith from the inception of the project to the splendid fulfilment, and send our very warm thanks and congratulations to all concerned.

"Our last general meeting was devoted to reports on the School. Each speaker had been detailed to report on a specific day and, as far as was possible in one evening, salient points from all lectures and some snappy impressions of Summer School personalities were included. Interest was so evident that time has been set aside at next Wednesday's meeting for discussion and questions, which we expect to range from points on Mr. Coppard on the short story to 'what did they give you to eat?'

"I am to assure you of our whole-hearted support of the Writers Circles' Summer School 1950. We are eagerly awaiting the word 'Go' to start booking right away."

I make no apology for the fact that a very large proportion of this history is devoted to the first School.

Every School has been eventful, every School has had its highlights, but to catalogue them all would inevitably have made for monotonous reading. And it was that first School which set the pattern and the standard, and I feel that a full understanding of how "our" Swanwick came into being is essential to an appreciation of what it has been through those thirty-four years, still is today, and, God willing will continue to be.

How it all began and what has made it such an outstanding success that every year four or five hundred writers and would-be writers – professionals and amateurs – apply for the 325 places now available, is revealed in the story which follows.

1

Not even a Shoestring

It all began on Saturday, 12th June 1948, barely three years after the War in Europe ended. Cecil Hunt, the Chairman of the London Writer Circle, shortly to become its President, had felt the need for some kind of writers' school or conference as he spoke at writer circles' meetings in different parts of the country. Many were small in number, meeting in members' houses, sometimes with few, if any, professional writers to guide them in their attempts to achieve publication. Yet there were also circles with a bigger and more professional membership. Cecil Hunt wanted members of different circles to be brought together so that the enthusiasm and knowledge of the more successful could be passed on to those struggling to make the grade.

The committee of the London Writer Circle discussed the matter until it was decided to call a meeting of two delegates from each of the Writer Circles known to exist all over the country with the object of considering the possibility of starting a Writer Circles' Summer School.

That meeting was held on 12th June 1948 at the Institute of Journalists' Hall, 4, Tudor Street, London. There is no record of the number attending this gathering but, as I recall, there were about one hundred and twenty of us. We came from all parts of the country including Scotland, Ireland and Wales and the Isle of Man.

It was an all-day conference, commencing at 10.30, when Ian Hay, then President of the London Writer Circle, welcomed the delegates. Cecil Hunt presided throughout the day and Hugh Stephens, Secretary of the London Writer Circle, recorded the Minutes. Kenneth Myer, Editor of *The Writer*, a Hutchinson publication, was present to give his support.

The morning session was devoted to exploring the possibility of holding either a week-end or a week's Summer School for writers, to take place during 1949, while the afternoon sessions were addressed by Anthony Gilbert, the well-known crime writer, and Wilson Midgley, editor of *John o' London's Weekly*.

It was soon evident that the idea of organising a Writers' Summer School was worth pursuing and Donald Segar, a delegate from the Manchester Circle, proposed a resolution that: "A Summer School for writers be held in 1949 and that it be of a week's duration." Mr. J. McCormick (Rotherham Circle) seconded the proposal.

An amendment that "the additional facility of reduced fee for those only able to attend for the week-end be granted", was not adopted and the original resolution was carried.

Discussion followed concerning the venue, fee, conditions of membership, and the selection of a committee to organise the event. Kenneth Myer assured the meeting that *The Writer* would give all possible help if such a School was inaugurated, and it was understood that he was willing to serve as its secretary.

It is interesting to note that Swanwick was not even mentioned in the discussion on the venue, the main towns favoured by the vote of those present being Oxford, Cambridge or Bath, with the added suggestion of seeking accommodation in the universities of either of the first two towns. Finally the venue was left unresolved until investigation had been made.

It was decided that, if at all possible, the fee should be kept within the figure of $6\frac{1}{2}$ guineas per head for the whole period, this to include full board. This year (1983) the fee is £70 for six days, which is generally considered extremely good value by present standards. Not only inflation but also the vast improvements of facilities, furnishings and extensions to buildings at Swanwick have contributed to this dramatic change.

The Hayes. A view of the house and lawn.

Another point worth noting is that during the discussions concerning the month to be selected for the School to take place, all the summer months were mentioned, with August the least popular yet, in the event, that is the month during which it has been held in all years, with the exception of one, when it was held in July – but more concerning this later.

From the very beginning applications from writers who were not members of writers' circles were accepted, but it was agreed that members of circles should be given preference over others when allocating places.

Finally, a committee of five was appointed from the delegates attending the conference in June 1948, with power to co-opt others as necessary. Since those attending that conference were mostly unknown to each other, I have always felt the committee selected was chosen rather on a "hit and miss" basis, those who took most part in the discussion being elected to the committee, with their qualifications to perform the task unknown! Those elected were: Mrs. Lewis (Reading), Nancy Martin (Croydon), Elizabeth Walsh (Oxford), Bob Hunter (Vice Chairman of the London Writer Circle), and Donald Segar (Chairman of Manchester Circle). Cecil Hunt and Hugh Stephens, Chairman and Secretary of London Writer Circle, together with Kenneth Myer, were appointed ex-officio members of the committee.

We were all so caught up with the idea of having a Summer School for Writers that no one thought of asking where the initial funds were to come from to get the organisation under way. In the event the Summer School Secretary had to advance the sum of £10 to pay for the initial printing and correspondence with writer circles and others.

The first committee meeting is recorded in the Minute Book as taking place on Saturday, 2nd October 1948, at Tweedmount, Upper Shirley Road, Croydon, the home of the secretary, but Kenneth Myer did call the committee together very much earlier than this. As I remember, it was a completely informal meeting held in a small coffee shop in Paternoster Row, opposite Hutchinson's publishing house. Paternoster Row, close by St. Paul's, was a narrow road, famous for its publishers and second-hand bookshops, but the road and the bookshops have long since disappeared. The meeting was called for the purpose of informing the committee that Kenneth Myer could not undertake the Secretaryship of the School as Hutchinsons could not, or would not, provide him with a typist to do the work!

I remember sitting round a marble-topped table, drinking coffee as we heard the news that we were committed to organising the Summer School with no secretary to undertake the work. All members of the committee were present with the exception of the ex-officio members. Bob Hunter had already been appointed chairman of the organising committee and he asked every member in turn if they would take over the task of secretary. Each declined!

It began to look as though the School was a dead duck. I had already written several books for different publishers and, with a working husband who was home for all meals, and two daughters still at school, was engaged in writing my first book for Macmillans. However, in what might be regarded as a weak moment, and because I believed in the project, I volunteered for the job of secretary *pro tem*! I held the office for two years before relinquishing it, taking it over again for four years until Marjorie Harris accepted the position which she has held continuously since until the last School (1982) when she felt she could no longer serve in this capacity on account of failing eyesight. The fact that Marjorie has been secretary of such a successful event for so many years is sufficient indication of her business efficiency which has kept the organisation running so smoothly, while the manner in which the news that she was relinquishing the position was received is evidence of members' appreciation of her value to the School. Further reference to this is made on page 92.

In the early days (of 1948/49), the committee consisted of a small group of writers living in different parts of the country, none of whom had any prior experience of organising a Writers' School. To the best of my knowledge such an event had never been held anywhere in this country by any writers' organisation. Now, as is well known, writers' conferences and courses are held regularly in many places, most having been started as a result of Swanwick's success. None are as big or as widely known as the Writers' Summer School, where upwards of 350 people, including lecturers, officers and committee now attend each year.

First we sent letters to all the writer circles which were then listed in *The Writer* informing them of the proposed school and inviting them to contribute gifts or loans of money towards the initial expense. The response was small by any standard but especially so considering the project to be planned. We received £15.13s.6d. in donations and £19.6s.6d. in loans – a total of £35 contributed by a very small number of circles.

Looking back on it all I marvel that we had the audacity to go ahead and plan the first school on such slender resources. Was it sheer doggedness or blind faith?

It had been left to me, following that informal meeting in Paternoster Row, to find a suitable centre at which to hold the School. Remembering the proposal to keep the fee within $6\frac{1}{2}$ guineas, I tried a variety of possible places, such as boarding schools in different parts of the country which I knew were made available for conferences during the long summer break. Their terms were reasonable but no staff would be available to assist us and although kitchens with cooking facilities were included in the terms, we would have to find our own caterers. Universities were not available at the terms we could afford.

It was then, in May 1948, that Marjorie Harris rang me. "Have you tried Swanwick?" she asked.

I knew of this conference centre 13 miles north of Derby, but had always understood that it was used only for religious conferences. Marjorie, however, thought it was worth trying. A phone call elicited the response that there was just one week still available in the summer months of 1949. It was the period 22nd to 28th August – Monday to Sunday. If we were prepared to book the whole place, and not share it with another party, the rate would be 14s.6d. per day per person, inclusive of all meals.

This was certainly the best offer so far, but then came the question of numbers. It was necessary to guarantee an attendance of 200 or pay the agreed rate per day for any short-fall from that number. It was anybody's guess how many writers would attend and at that stage in the proceedings there was no possibility of finding out. The less optimistic thought there might be no more than 70!

We took the risk and signed the guarantee! This is what Bob Hunter had in mind when he said, at a business meeting of the whole School, that the Writers' Summer School was founded on faith, hope and courage.

I still have copies of the budget as estimated, by my husband, Leslie Salmon, on my behalf. This was presented to the Committee on 2nd October 1948, more than ten months before the date of the first summer school, before a programme had been arranged, lecturers contacted, before registration forms had been printed or any monies received beyond that £35 from Writer Circles!

The relevant Minute is worth recording: *"Budget of Expenses and Income.* Details of estimated expenses and income, based on an attendance of 200, 300 or 400 had been prepared by the Secretary and were circulated among the committee for consideration. Based on executive expenses totalling £275, and an attendance of 200, with a consequent cost for accommodation of £870, making the total estimated expenses for a summer school of 200 members £1,145, it was agreed that a charge of £6 per person for the period would be satisfactory. . . . It was further agreed that this charge should include sports, and transport between Derby and Swanwick provided members could fit in with the coach time-table. The committee decided to charge a registration fee of 35s.0d., the balance of the fee being payable about a fortnight before the commencement of the School."

What a risk we took, but it was a calculated risk. After 28 cancellations had been received 258 members attended that first School and we made a profit of £191.17s.6d. after refunding the gifts as well as the loans made by writer circles.

Our faith was justified by the financial result, which

was important. Even more important was the actual value of the School to those 258 writers who were present at this so recent prisoner of war camp which had not yet recovered from the austerity of those years. The School's purpose, as stated on every programme since its inception, has been: "To provide a meeting place for writers where, amidst congenial surroundings, they may give and receive help and encouragement in the art of writing."

How far this was achieved in that first year and every year since can be judged from the events recorded in the following pages.

Marjorie Harris aptly expressed the feelings of the other three first-year members, who are still associated with the School, when she said: "The outstanding feature was friendship. I had the feeling then of 'belonging', as if to a special sect, a Swanwick society. The germ was sown then and has grown ever since."

What, then, happened in August 1949 to justify such a remark and to cause so many of those who have been there since, to talk about "the magic of Swanwick"? And what was Swanwick like in those earlier days?

2

The Magic of Swanwick

The Hayes Conference Centre at Swanwick, in Derbyshire, is described today as "probably the largest of its kind in Europe. It is privately owned and is directed by representatives of organisations which both own and regularly use the place." An illustrated brochure gives its position as being "central for the British Isles, near the M1 (No. 28), two miles from Alfreton and Mansfield Parkway Station, and 13 miles from Derby. It is half an hour by private coach and motorway from East Midland Airport and under three hours from London Heathrow."

Having tentatively reserved a week for the first Writers' Summer School to be held there, Cecil Hunt agreed to inspect the place to ascertain its suitability for the purpose. He found it to be a large mansion on a 70-acre estate, surrounded by barbed wire, with views of slag heaps remaining from open-cast mines. The mansion itself had not yet recovered from its wartime condition, but new management was being installed at the time of the visit and the premises, with the large dining room, garden room and conference hall capable of seating more than 300, though plain in decoration and furnishing were, Cecil reported, adequate, and there were several sitting rooms. The bedroom accommodation also was sufficient for our purpose. I do not remember that he reported on the adequacy of bathrooms and toilets, but it was probably a good thing that he did not and that no woman member of the committee inspected the place beforehand. Had we done so we might have looked more closely at the iron bedsteads, with their sagging springs and flock mattresses. We should also have had considerable doubt about the communal washing facilities and the inadequate number of toilets, but Cecil Hunt must have felt something of the atmosphere, even at that time when the place was unoccupied, with no conference in progress, for there is, as we were soon to discover, something about The Hayes which is unique.

None would have dared to hope that, from the very first year of the School, and for the next thirty-three years, members would be talking about the magic of Swanwick. Yet, since starting to write this history, I have received many letters from past and present members referring to it in those terms. More than one wrote of "the happiness that is Swanwick", a statement of fact that most of those who have attended throughout the years would endorse.

How did this happen? Broadly speaking, through the dedication and enthusiasm of that small first committee and its officers and the easy friendliness of those famous writers who agreed to lecture without a fee, and particularly through the marvellous co-operation and untiring energy of Wally Milne – only that year appointed Manager of The Hayes – with his equally untiring and happy staff who welcomed us warmly. They quickly became our friends, some remaining to welcome us for many more years. There were then and still are, Mr. Winspear, Wally's deputy and accountant, and Miss Williams, who brought us our early morning tea with a smile and her own weather forecast! That was before self-service was inaugurated, with numerous electric kettles and necessary supplies. These good folk are still there, though time is passing and retirement must necessarily draw near for many of them, as it did for Winnie and Mr. Maudlin.

But what of the place – the estate itself? In the course of a long article published in *The Freelance Writer and*

Photographer (now defunct), under the heading *The First Summer School for writers was a great success*, Hugh Stephens, publicity officer of the first School, wrote: "The Hayes, which incidently has housed many conferences in its time, is a delightful old-world mansion, capable of accommodating up to 400 persons, set among some of the most beautiful scenery in the country. During the 1939–45 fracas it also housed high-ranking German officers and evidence of its being a prisoner-of-war camp is still visible in remnants of barbed wire barriers and occasional notices which announce that such and such a place is 'verboten'."

Mary Uncles, who has attended most Schools over the years from 1949 onwards, and was present last year (1982) records: "We still had our ration books and the effects of Spartan living were still with us in that first Summer School. I don't think anyone who wasn't there could imagine the scene in the Garden House, the long uncarpeted corridors, the iron beds and rush mats beside them. You could see the strange sight of women carrying ewers of water to replenish the bowls on the rickety dressing tables.

"But there was still the atmosphere. I can't explain it, but it seemed to those of us who gathered there that we knew something exciting would come of this venture.

"There was the Swanwick ghost, of course. I had no idea The Hayes had been a prisoner-of-war camp, although barbed wire at the back of the Garden House should have suggested this. The very first night I dreamed I saw a soldier wearing a helmet, standing by my dressing table. Only later did I hear other people's tales. Constance Dearden, in much later years, when the Garden House was pink-carpeted, heard steps in heavy boots on uncarpeted stairs. When she looked round there was no one. Last year a lady informed me she heard heavy marching feet at 5.30 a.m. throughout the week's stay. No doubt the hidden tunnel had unearthed its ghosts!"

Swanwick has a history of being used during two world wars. Taken over as barracks during the First World War in 1914, the Secretary was instructed by the Board that he could continue to accept bookings for 1915, adding a note to all letters of acceptance that "the War Office is aware that the estate will be required for conferences during the next season". As the Company is reported to have made a profit of £2,000 during the financial year ended October 1915, it can be assumed that the War Office only temporarily occupied the centre.

As already indicated, the situation was different during the Second World War when The Hayes was first used by the War Office to accommodate British troops, but was later converted to a prisoner-of-war camp for German Air Force officers – a fact which will go down in the annals of history, for it was from The Hayes that one German officer finally escaped.

Stuart Drinkwater, who has attended most Swanwicks, describing it as "the annual happiness that is Swanwick", is an inveterate browser amongst the second-hand bookstalls. He has sent me information about a book published jointly by William Collins and Michael Joseph and entitled *The One that Got Away*, the authors being Kendal Burt and James Leasor. It is the fascinating story of Oberleutnant Franz von Werra, who made a daring and adventurous escape from The Hayes. The authorities at the Conference Centre knew the story well; they knew that, in 1940, five prisoners escaped by means of a tunnel, started in a disused room in the north wing of the Garden House, but no one had been able to locate it. In August 1981, Wally Milne met the committee when we arrived as the advance party to prepare for the influx of members the next day. The only way to describe him on that occasion is that he was like an overgrown schoolboy!

"We've located the tunnel," he said excitedly. "Come and see."

And, heedless of the dinner bell, he led us to the spot near the Garden House where a hole was revealed through the bank around the new foundations which had been prepared for further bathroom and toilet accommodation. The hole was only just big enough for a man to wriggle through.

"There it is," said Wally, and went on to explain how the prisoners had dug out the tunnel with a short-handled scoop provided by the War Office to deal with incendiary bombs, disposing of the earth quite a distance from the spot. The tunnel ran underneath a double security barbed wire fence and out on to farmland. It had taken forty years to discover its whereabouts.

Another memento of these prisoners, Ruth Bagnall informs me, is a painted Triptych of the Nativity, which can be seen in Swanwick Church. This is the work of an artist prisoner. He did the three paintings, and other officers paid to have it mounted. The finished work was presented to the vicar at the time who was chaplain to the camp and helpful to the prisoners. The children depicted at the crib were the artist's own children, painted from photographs he had carried on him to the prison.

The Hayes was built in the 1850's/60's by the Wright family and sold in 1910 by Fitzherbert Wright to a newly-formed company known as the First Conference Estate Limited, for £11,500, about one-fifth of what it had cost the Wright family to build some fifty or sixty years previously. It is this company which runs it today, but it has had its financial problems for I am informed that, at one period, the Company's shares were changing hands at two shillings each.

Many conversions and additions had to take place before The Hayes could be used as a conference centre. The hunting stables were converted to what is now the Quadrangle, the Garden House was built to hold two hundred people – all bedroom accommodation – and the present big dining room was added to the side of the kitchen wall of the original house. The Chapel was built in 1932 at a cost of £1,700, all but £200 of this being donated by two interested people.

Since that time, of course, and over the years we have been using the conference centre, very many improvements, additions and changes have been made. In fact, every year there is something more to see – extra bedrooms, an additional sound-proofed dining room, more conference rooms, additional sanitary accommodation – for Wally Milne is a manager with ideas and the energy and foresight to carry them out.

An interesting fact is that Lilian Daykin, a delightful elderly member, who had her first children's book published by Harrap as a result of that first Summer School, used to be invited to Christmas parties at The Hayes when the Wrights lived there and she was a young child, for her father was a miner and the owners of The Hayes were in the coal-mining business.

3

Faith, Hope and Courage

Although at the first informal meeting in Paternoster Row the committee appeared so inadequate for the task, its members were soon determined to do everything in their power to make the venture a success. All would have agreed that this was largely due to the keenness, dedication and business ability of Cecil Hunt who, although under medical restraint, attended every committee meeting and proved himself to be a very wise counsellor and friend. The Writers Circles' Summer School was his brain child and he set himself to develop it on good sound principles. What was more, he inspired us all to do the same.

My husband and I were then living in Shirley, Surrey, within a few miles of Addington Hills. To save time and travelling expense we held our committee meetings at our house for the whole day, on three Saturdays – in October, January and May, only stopping for lunch at the restaurant on the Hills. We did have the opportunity to make final arrangements at The Hayes by spending two nights there immediately prior to the opening of the School. With only the Chairman having seen the place previously this was essential that we might become acquainted with the management and staff, adjust plans for bedroom accommodation and group meetings, make arrangements for sales of authors' books in the book room, put up necessary notices, lists of members, etc. There was plenty to do but I well remember a very pleasant interlude when we were invited to afternoon tea on the lawn at the Manager's house which is situated near the entrance to the grounds. This enabled us to form a firm basis of friendship with Wally, his charming wife and their delightful small family, a friendship which has remained and been strengthened over the years.

But a good deal of planning was done during those three full days of committee meetings before we ever went to Swanwick, while the secretarial work involved was tremendous. Approximately one thousand registration forms were despatched with covering letters, and about two thousand additional letters were sent out.

It was a great relief to me, as secretary, when a very able member of Croydon Writers' Circle – Pauline Randell – offered to give free secretarial assistance during the busiest period. None of us received or even thought of an honorarium in those days, although, at the first Annual General Meeting held at the School it was agreed that Pauline should receive £15 for her assistance, and honoraria of twenty-five guineas and ten guineas were voted to the Secretary and Treasurer respectively, and it was agreed that honoraria should be granted to these two officers in future.

Although the number now attending the School has increased by about one hundred, lecturers and members alike constantly express their amazement at the efficient and smooth manner in which the school operates. But in those days it was something quite new to us all and we were feeling our way, not knowing what to expect. It has been interesting to compare the registration forms, circular letters and programmes used over the years and to discover that, basically, they have changed little from those produced during the earliest years. Even the sketch for the block of the main house we occupy, which was produced by a well-known Croydon artist – Cyril Spackman, who was a founder member of Croydon Writers' Circle – is still being used. I think we can justifiably claim that the continuing progress and success of the Summer School owes much to the fact that firm and satisfactory foundations were laid in those early, unpredictable years.

Although, initially, we had no funds and therefore no need of a Treasurer, it was obvious that a large sum of money would have to be handled if the venture was a success. The Treasurer of the London Writer Circle was unable to undertake the task, but Brian Sutton, a London bank official, and well-tried Treasurer of Croydon Writers' Circle, was willing to keep the books although, he informed us, he would not be able to attend the School. However, we knew him and his abilities well and as Leslie had already been appointed Social Secretary and Transport Officer, and it was on his estimate of possible income and expenditure that the School fee had been based, it was agreed he should take over as Cashier at the School. Brian Sutton, therefore, was appointed Treasurer and this proved a very satisfactory arrangement for that first year.

We were fortunate in our choice of a host. Sydney Goldsack, then the well-known Sales Director of William Collins, not only consented to be the first Host of the School, but attended the committee meetings in January and May, inviting us to be his guests at lunch at the restaurant on the Hills. He became as keen about the School as we were and although he came only that first year, constantly afterwards he enquired about its progress.

One of the very big advantages of having Sydney as Host was that we were able to invite some of the best-known authors of that period. They were Collins authors and only had to be told that their Sales Director was Host to get their agreement to lecture and stay for several days; some enjoyed it so much that they stayed for the whole period. Thus the programme for the first Summer School contains the names of A. E. Coppard, John Brophy, Helena Grose, John Moore, Marguerite Steen and Noel Streatfeild, each of whom, in addition to giving excellent and informative lectures, entered into the spirit of the School, as will be seen in a later chapter. Then there was Trevor Allen who, shortly afterwards, became Chairman of the London Writer Circle, a position which he held until last year, when he retired after serving in that office for twenty-one years.

At Swanwick my husband became known as "the backroom boy", for he always seemed to be available to answer innumerable questions and do any job which was needed, whether it was to help members find their rooms, accept the care of lost property and discover the rightful owners, give out necessary notices as required, or take over arrangements for excursions and social activities.

The 1950 Committee. Nancy Martin, front left. Leslie Salmon, leaning on flower stand.

In those days petrol was scarce and there were no cheap railway fares. It was Leslie's idea that we should hire coaches to bring people from London to The Hayes. This proved to be very popular and is a practice which has continued each year since, even though, with many more members travelling by car, the small area of garage space is quickly utilised and a long line of vehicles extends down the parking spaces on the drive.

In the first two years we hired three coaches from what was then the Maidstone and District Coach Company, who quoted the most competitive terms. They not only brought eighty-eight members from Victoria Coach Station right up the long drive to the house, but coaches and drivers remained for the whole period, the three drivers being accommodated at The Hayes, and we were able to use them for the two half-day excursions, merely being charged the extra cost of petrol. In the light of the present inflationary figures, the return fare charged to members for their journey between London and The Hayes, namely £2.1s.0d., seems ridiculously cheap, especially as this included lunch on both journeys as well as gratuities to the drivers and waiters. Furthermore, the individual charge to members for each of the two coach excursions was only 7s.6d. inclusive of entrance fees to places of interest; small wonder that Wally Milne told me that our percentage of administrative charges covered by the fee to members compares most favour-ably with that charged by other organisations.

Yet the financial statement for the 1949 School shows the total cost of transport to be £263.0s.5d., with receipts of £260.15s.0d, revealing a small loss on transport of £2.5s.5d., this having covered the return journey between London and Swanwick as well as excursions! One cannot get much nearer than that when estimating possible costs! Since that was the year when, starting with no funds at all, we made an overall profit of £191.17s.6d. after repaying loans *and donations* from Writers' Circles, members had every reason to be satisfied with the fee of £6 for their six-day stay at The Hayes. There was, therefore, a reasonable sum to cover initial expenses for the next School without the need for loans or donations.

Marjorie Harris, not then free to serve on the committee but a very strong and willing supporter, recalls the first journey to Swanwick in the London Coach: "My first memory, after the School had actually materialised, is of sitting alone in a fleet of three coaches, careering up the Old Kent Road to Victoria Coach Station to collect members for Swanwick. What an exciting journey it was. When we stopped for lunch at the Grand Hotel in Northampton, it was extraordinary how many people had to shop for this and that and they got lost in the process."

She adds: "The first School seems a very long time ago after running so many Schools since. Nevertheless, the first one undoubtedly had something which has never quite been repeated. We were all fresh from the frustrations of the war, and the School was grasped as a new experience, almost as though we had been let out of school."

That was obviously how our Chairman felt, for one of the things which stands out in my mind is of a fine summer night – the night before everyone arrived – when, having more or less finalised our preparations, Cecil Hunt led us on a tour round the grounds. He was so excited at the prospect of the successful event planned to start the next day, and the fact that he was temporarily free from medical restraint, that, like a young schoolboy just home for the holidays, he went skipping down the path towards the duck pond!

Small wonder that Cecil's arrangement to meet members for private talks about their writing problems was always in the same place. In fact, "Meet me at the duck pond," became a Swanwick cliché!

So – the scene was set – play was about to begin!

4

The First Great Arrival

It was three o'clock in the afternoon of Monday, 22nd August 1949 – a date to be remembered – the first day of the first Writers Circles' Summer School. The morning dawned bright with intermittent bursts of sunshine; the forecast was good and our spirits were high.

The big table from the entrance hall had been moved outside the front doors. Two of us were seated at it facing down the drive, pens poised, lists and papers at the ready as the coaches which had brought train travellers from Derby station came into view. Other members of the committee, together with some stalwart men who had arrived early, were standing ready to help with luggage and give a warm welcome to those who were to make the School come alive.

It was our job to collect ration books from members as they arrived. We emphasised the necessity not only to bring ration books with coupons available for six days' rations, but to have them ready in handbags or pockets. It was our intention to ensure that no one entered the house without first giving up their ration book. Few had forgotten to bring them but quite a number had to admit that they were locked in their cases for safe keeping. Rather than risk confusion by having cases opened in the drive we kept a note of such members, letting them through on the firm understanding that their books would be brought to the office later that afternoon.

One rather amusing memory I have is of a few members who approached clutching small packets of tea, sugar and other rationed goods, explaining that they had used their coupons to purchase rations for the family at home before leaving, so had brought their share in kind! Fortunately they were few in number or the management could have been faced with odd chops of different kinds of meat, small bags of tea and sugar, and dollops of butter which had melted on the journey.

It was easy enough to cope with those who arrived in small numbers, but had we not arranged each of the advance party's duties down to the last detail, and had we not all made ourselves fully acquainted with the positioning of bedrooms, bathroom and toilet accommodation, the welcome could have ended in confusion. Endless were the questions asked and answered. There were those who could not locate their luggage, only to discover they had not recognised it among the rest. More serious at first appeared to be the complaints from a few that they had found somebody else's luggage in their room! Had we double-booked any rooms? But no! This proved to result from one or other of the two having misread the number of their room or, in some cases, taken a room of the same number in the Quadrangle when they should have been in the Garden House.

There were a few grumbles, as there must be when there are people of all ages, coming from many different backgrounds. I can still see the smartly dressed woman who came to complain that there was a spider in her bedroom and the room had not been thoroughly cleaned. She declared she would not have brought her best clothes and fur coat had she known what the place was like! She wanted to claim the return of her fee as she must go home the next day. She didn't get her money back and she didn't return the next day but settled down and enjoyed her stay.

There were those who informed us that they were suffering from a heart problem and had been given a room on the third floor of the Garden House! Useless to say they should have informed us of their weakness when registering, although, with the place full to capacity, it was a major task to swop to suit everyone. Somehow all problems were solved and we breathed a sigh of relief when at last the seats on the covered terrace and those around the lawns were filled with happy, smiling people of all ages, drinking tea and enjoying the home-made bread, rock cakes and gingerbread for which The Hayes is famous. The buzz of conversation was such as is heard when people of like interests get together. Friendships were already being made, many of which were to last for a very long time.

This continued over dinner, when the big dining hall was filled with members at long tables cheerfully passing along plates of food served from very large dishes by members seated at the end of each table. While this was in progress the friendly voice of the Manager, Wally Milne – to become so familiar during the days and years which followed – was heard for the first time welcoming the members of the School and distilling useful information with a good deal of wit.

Marjorie Harris writes: "My main recollection of that first evening is of masses of members filling every corner of the then smaller Hayes. Oh, it was crowded! The noise was colossal, especially in the dining room – since sound-proofed – where we sat in close proximity to house everybody. Early morning the Garden House corridors were filled with queues of people waiting for bathrooms, or escaping from those hard mattresses, but still anxious to continue discussions after their short night. We seemed to have practically no sleep during that first Spartan Swanwick; besides, everything was much too exciting. Never was there so much talk!"

By the time the School started, Harold Harris had become Managing Editor of *The Writer*. He became much involved with the School and organised a competition for a thousand-word article calculated to be of help to writers who were not there. Victor Allan, a much-travelled writer who had written short stories, poems, articles and an anthology of East Anglian literature, won the prize of five guineas. His article was printed in the October issue of *The Writer* and I quote from it not only because it sums up so adequately the spirit and purpose of that first Summer School – a spirit and purpose which were to characterise all future schools – but because it is written by one not involved with the inner workings of it, as we on the committee were. These are the views of one who came fresh from outside – "in from the cold" – and so express unbiased opinions of its values.

The opening paragraph reads: "The roads and railways converging upon Derby brought nearly three hundred men and women writers to a common meeting-place in the Mansion and park of The Hayes at Swanwick. They came from all parts of the British Isles, and some from far beyond, and there was a sense of pilgrimage in their coming. Of widely diverse types and ages and levels of achievement, they travelled across England that day to testify, like pilgrims of old, to the validity of beliefs and ideals shared by all. There, before a hand was joined or a word spoken, were the seals of the unique fellowship we were to find in a few days, golden in the remembrance of so many who experienced them."

By 8.30 on the first night the conference hall was filled to capacity for the informal welcome meeting. No one could doubt the warmth of the welcome given by Sydney Goldsack, or the eager anticipation of the members as Cecil Hunt introduced his wife, Kathleen, who had been appointed information officer. He introduced the officers, committee and other helpers and spoke of the plans which had been made to enable everyone to enjoy themselves and to make the most of the opportunities afforded by the presence of so many well-known authors to give their expert advice and encouragement. Even the coffee queue which followed the meeting had its advantages, for that was just another of the opportunities for chat and the forming of friendships, as many have testified over the years.

To quote Mary Uncles again: "I feel I can drink my

coffee and, without glancing at the person beside me, fall at once into conversation. We all have the same common interest and it draws us together. There is a sense of moving forward, an aim always in view. This is not a week of light entertainment, to be forgotten on parting, but knowledge gained, to be treasured and worked at. . . ."

The end of the day, until a very late hour, saw groups of people drinking and talking animatedly together, while eventually the officers, committee and speakers relaxed in Room X, satisfied that all augured very well for a happy and profitable six days.

Yes – the Writers' Summer School was alive and well and the air was full of great expectations!

5

One Crowded Happy Week

"We are naturally proud of *The Writer*'s close connection with the beginning of a venture which came to fruition so triumphantly at Swanwick. . . . Only the writers who were there . . . can appreciate the full measure of success, but we have attempted in this and the following ten pages, to convey something of the variety, of the instruction, and of the spirit which characterised this great landmark in the Writer Circle movement."

So wrote Harold Harris in the opening page of the October issue of *The Writer*, a magazine alas, long defunct, but of great value to writers when it was published by Hutchinsons. He continues, in the same article: "Famous authors who had generously agreed to give a talk enjoyed themselves so much and themselves derived such benefit from other talks, that they stayed on. There were no cliques, no exclusiveness, no awkward moments when shy people wondered if they might be intruding on other people's conversation. For one glorious week we all talked shop from early morning till late at night.

"If, at mealtimes, you turned to discuss some problem with your neighbour, you might find yourself talking to an as yet unpublished poet or to one of our foremost short story writers. Your food might be brought to you by a junior reporter or one of Fleet Street's most successful free-lances, depending on who happened to be sitting at the serving end of your table."

Turning again to the winning entry in the competition

set by that magazine, Victor Allan expresses the feelings of most of the members who were there: "They were crowded days, in which the tempo of life quickened suddenly to the beat of a virile, challenging note. Time seemed to run through a sieve, as it does for so many of us, and was directed into the productive channels chiselled by a forethought and organisation beyond praise.

"In twelve lectures every branch of the writer's work – from technical and pictorial journalism to the art of the short story, the novel, radio drama and the children's book – was dealt with by a master of his or her craft. What more valuable privilege for young writers than to have before them, day after day, such speakers as A. E. Coppard, John Brophy, Marguerite Steen, Noel Streatfeild, Helena Grose – to name but a few – as the targets of quickfire questions from all quarters of a packed conference hall?

"Under the firm and sympathetic chairmanship of Cecil Hunt, quick to discern and encourage the hesitant questioner, how many doubts and problems were resolved in the course of those comradely interchanges between lecturer and audience! Interchanges which, as the week progressed, were continued more individually at our meal tables or in walks among the lawns and shrubberies, when men and women who had mounted the hard road to a place in the sun came back for a while to lend a hand of guidance and encouragement to those who knew only its stones and obstacles.

"What did it all mean to the writer striving to establish a niche for himself and his work? It would be impossible to enumerate the fine points of craftsmanship, the practicalities of method, technique and marketing, the viewpoint of editor and publisher confided so freely by the masters to the guildsmen of their craft.

"Words come back at random, borne on the fresh wind which blows through the mind after Swanwick. Thus, Mr. Coppard's exposition of a pattern: 'For extraordinary characters the ordinary episode will do. But for ordinary characters the extraordinary episode must be found.'

"Or, Miss Streatfeild's reassurance that the supposed craving of children for violence is nonsense. Excitement, yes – but never the glorification of the villain. The kind of excitement the child likes best is that which comes from the daily life of the child.

"Again, Mr. Brophy, speaking of the novel: 'More should be left to the subconscious, let the theme lie fallow, neither commencing to write too soon when it is new, nor too late when it is over-ripe.'

"There were invaluable discussions – by Patricia Meredith on the requirements of the group of women's journals which she represented, by Cynthia Pugh on those of the drama department of the B.B.C., and by Sydney Goldsack and John Benn, who, speaking as directors of eminent publishing houses, gave generously of their experience and advice.

"In smaller discussion groups poets gained instruction from an aggregate of individual experience in the merchandising of their chancy wares and playwrights learnt of the clamorous demand by the Women's Institute movement for short plays with all-women casts – and women no longer young!"

Group discussions became a feature of each school, increasing in number as the years progressed. Two workshops were started, followed by courses on different aspects of writing for various media. These have continued to be an important part of the programme and are very popular, as are the panels on such subjects as "The Business Side of Writing", "Experts Advise", etc. Most lecturers who are available take a large part in these, and are always generous in their sharing of experience.

From the very beginning a full programme was arranged. In that first year it was customary to have two lectures in the morning and one in the evening, so anxious were we to make the most of the well-established writers who were our guests. Originally afternoons were devoted to sports, games or excursions to places of interest. There were organised tennis and cricket matches, clock golf and swimming with two afternoons for excursions. In 1952 the second coach excursion was dropped and games became less and less organised, members expressing the wish for more sessions of a practical nature rather than time to relax and enjoy the countryside! Thus, although many went home somewhat exhausted after rushing from one session to another during those early years, so anxious were they not to miss any bit of wisdom that would take them further on the road to success, there has continued to be a great demand for a full practical programme. Most members have now learned to be more selective than they were originally when it was a new experience to be given the opportunity of meeting with and gaining knowledge from such a variety of well-known writers who, previously, had been names on book jackets, on screen or television, or in newspapers and magazines.

Dancing has always been a popular part of the evening's entertainment although now, with many discussion groups continuing until a late hour, it starts at a much later hour, usually about eleven o'clock and continues until one in the morning! This has been made possible by the availability of the additional, though slightly smaller, assembly hall built in the grounds.

Exhausted though we may be at the conclusion of each School, press reports and the appreciative letters received from those who attend year by year, or for the first time, give ample testimony to the practical value of the whole thing.

Frank Knight, one of Croydon Writers' Circle's successful authors, is quoted as saying: "We started to talk on the coaches as they left Victoria for the Summer School, we talked through the week and were still talking when we left the coaches at Victoria on our return."

Again I quote Victor Allan, who sums it all up in the following words: "It is one of the burdens of the writer that much of his work must be done in a solitude of mind often peopled by spectres of doubt, disappointment and despair. It is not easy to find many to whom he can open his heart, and harder still to discover that hammer-and-anvil impact of mind upon mind from which fly the sparks of inspiration and imagination.

"In thousands of friendly talks at Swanwick, over tea cups in the canteen, on expeditions afoot and by coach over the Derbyshire hills, on paths which traversed gardens, lakeside and ripening orchards, between the dances on a summer night, when the radiance from lighted windows brought a touch of eighteenth-century grace to the formality of terrace and lawn – on those countless occasions, as many lanterns were lit. The timid found poise and confidence; the self-assured proportion and balance; the cynic a new infusion of faith and fellowship, and to all came the heartening reassurance that the enduring values of craftsmanship and critical appreciation are still supreme in the world of art and letters.

"That the Summer School gained hourly in stature and significance none there present could deny. That it will attain a widening significance and prestige in years to come few are likely to doubt."

6

Gala Night

"Mayor Gives Reception to 250 British Writers."

So read the headline in the *Derby Evening Telegraph* of 24th August 1949 while, two days later, the *Derbyshire Advertiser* – the County newspaper – reported the six-day event with full accounts of some of the lectures. The report on the Tuesday evening reception reads: "The delegates were welcomed by the Mayor and Mayoress of Derby (Alderman and Mrs. C. F. Bowmer) who shook hands with every writer at a civic reception and dance.

"Addressing the assembly on behalf of the borough and county, Alderman Bowmer said, 'Derbyshire is proud of its historic associations and I hope you will find inspiration in its rich folk-lore and in the dales for which we are famous.'"

The event was first proposed by the Summer School Committee at their meeting held on 22nd January 1949, the relevant Minute reading: "It was provisionally agreed that the Mayor and Mayoress of Derby be invited to dinner on Tuesday evening, August 23rd, to officially welcome the guests to Derbyshire. A proposal was that the evening's proceedings should conclude with a dance."

At that time, however, we had no idea of the importance of the decision then made, for it proved to be an outstanding evening – one which had such glamour that those who were present would never forget. The management and staff entered into the spirit of the evening with enthusiasm in spite of the additional work

42

it involved for them. As soon as lunch was finished that day the staff set to work clearing the big dining room and putting a high polish on the floor ready for the dance. A five-piece band had been engaged and the piano had to

The Hayes. A view towards the Vinery.

be transported by strong and willing men from the sitting room to the far end of the dining room. Chairs were placed all round the walls and the Garden Room leading into the dining room was cleared to accommodate the long table on which the buffet was to be set out. And what a buffet it was! As Mary Uncles wrote later: "In spite of austerity rations we had the most marvellous spread," while Noel Streatfeild was heard to remark:

"We couldn't put on such a display at a London hotel in these days."

It should, perhaps, be explained that much of the food was home-grown, while the chef gloried in being set free to make delicious confections to his heart's content. And for all this the additional sum charged by the Management of The Hayes, as well as the cost of the band, was covered without any extra charge to the members above that already paid!

A report of this event in the *Freelance Writer and Photographer* stated: "The evening started with all present mustering on the landing over the Great Hall where Hugh Stephens, acting as M.C. for the evening, shepherded them down the main staircase where each one was announced by Cecil Hunt and received by the Mayor of Derby and Mrs. Bowmer. This impressive ceremony over, all made their way to the Ballroom, where, to the tuneful music of Billy Smart's Band, dancing was continued to a late hour. A feature of the event was the magnificent buffet put on by the Manager and his ever-willing staff."

Mary Uncles continues her account of the event: "We were actually *presented*. It was like Buckingham Palace. We 'appeared' on the stairs and, like debs, did our little curtsey. No one knew then what we had written, or not written. We were all equal in anonymity!"

Those who could not, or did not, wish to dance played whist or simply sat chatting. It amuses me now to see printed on those early programmes "Dress optional" but fortunately no one took this literally! In fact, the splendid evening dresses and exotic shawls of the ladies and the dinner suits or evening dress of the men added considerable glamour to the occasion. Not surprisingly it was repeated in the years immediately following, but without the mayoral presence. Only last year Wally Milne said he wished it could be revived now, but he would not like to have to move the piano again!

The atmosphere, so frequently talked about, was

already there, but it seemed to take on a new dimension – for it was an occasion when tongues were unloosed even by the normally shy members, and friendships were cemented which, in many cases, were to last for a very long time.

It is this basic friendliness which has been the hallmark of Swanwick throughout the years. This is why it is important that, however difficult it is to find places for all who wish to attend each year, we must never purposely keep out those who have been often, for they have caught the spirit of Swanwick and while they are present the atmosphere will never evaporate.

Afterwards the great clearing-up began. It was not until the early hours of the morning that this started, and when Wally called for volunteers to help remove the piano and put up and lay the tables ready for breakfast, there was no lack of response from members and lecturers alike. In an incredibly short time the room looked as though the evening's festivities had never happened.

Then came another call from Wally. "Ice cream in the kitchen for all helpers!" And we all flocked into the big kitchen and swopped stories with everyone while the ice cream speedily disappeared.

7

Snippets and Fragments

Can writing be taught? Some years ago I was involved in two of a series of radio programmes entitled *Working with Words*. Three of us – the others being a well-known journalist and an equally well-known poet – were to discuss this question. The producer had invited me to take part because of my long association with the Writers' Summer School.

While there is a sense in which writing cannot be taught, no one who has any knowledge of Swanwick and its effects could deny that a great deal can be learnt from other successful writers. That many believe it can is evident from the number of people who attend creative writing courses and conferences of writers which take place all over the country. Evidence of this is seen in the letters and tributes which have been received from members telling of their achievements as a result of coming to Swanwick. But perhaps the most tangible evidence is the many "first books" which have appeared in the Book Room, followed, in a great many cases, by others from the same authors appearing year by year.

From the very beginning, authors attending the School have had their books on sale in the Book Room, organised and staffed by the management at The Hayes. These have a ready sale, as do those of our lecturers, with queues of purchasers wanting autographs. Titles range from the big literary biographies by outstanding authors to the small-sized paperbacks; from books on technical subjects to DIY; from books for young people to children's picture books; from plays to poetry. Much

46

space has had to be devoted to romantic novels of all kinds, a section which has grown considerably over the years as Swanwick members have achieved success in this genre.

Since being asked to write this history of the School I have received a great many letters enumerating successes as a result of attending at Swanwick. I cannot include them all, but must quote the delightful story that came from Rhona Martin (no relation). She writes: "I had my life changed by the Summer School before I ever saw Swanwick. In 1976 I tried – and failed – to get a place; in 1977 I tried again, and 'my other half', not wanting to be left alone in the house while I went, said – 'Put me on the list with you', which, in my ignorance of procedure, I did, and we were both put on the waiting list. He got in and I did not! However, he found his first Swanwick so exciting that he returned with two apparently unconnected pieces of news: the first was that a prize for a historical novel was being set up in memory of Georgette Heyer (that was all he remembered about it), and the second was that he, being Hungarian, had got into conversation with Diane Pearson of Corgi, who had been talking about her novel *Czardas*, and that he had told her I had just finished a historical novel and she had consented to look at it.

"I dismissed the idea of entering my beginner's work for a competition and, in my greenhorn innocence imagining that paperback publication was less ambitious than hardback, decided to submit it to Diane. I had no idea that she was connected with the Georgette Heyer prize, so you can imagine my astonishment when I received her letter telling me that she was impressed with *Gallows Wedding* and that she advised me to consider it entered for the competition, adding that she had already passed it to Jill Black of the Bodley Head and they had agreed it should go on to the short list! After three more weeks of nailbiting the incredible news came that it had won, and I knew I was on my way at last.

"In fact, it was not until 1979 that I actually got a place at Swanwick, and it leads me to wonder whether anyone else has had his or her life profoundly affected by Swanwick without actually having been there."

There is another outcome to this story, for Rhona Martin has experienced no difficulty in getting a place at the School for the last two years, for she was asked to lead a discussion group on "Characterisation" and give a talk on "Tackling Your Second Novel".

I must, however, add a warning note here lest our lecturers should suffer from unsolicited manuscripts being thrust at them while they are at the School. This is actively discouraged. In Rhona's case the lecturer *asked* to see it.

Another example of a step up the success ladder is that of Rae Shirley, a Welsh member who is one of the four who were at the first Summer School and has attended and taken part in many since. She writes: "In 1952 I won my first playwriting competition at Swanwick. L. du Garde Peach was the adjudicator and the prize was a rehearsal of my play, *Blue are the Hills*, on the stage at the famous Barn Theatre at Great Hucklow. Although I have since won over eighty competitions, and am now published in this country and the States, that first heady experience of seeing my work staged by a professional producer will always remain one of my happiest memories."

(There was in fact a packed audience, for an excursion was planned from Swanwick to witness the production at Great Hucklow at the invitation of L. du Garde Peach, who was our delightful and informative host.)

"And now John, my son, has become a devotee of Swanwick," continues Rae, "and I hope his future Swanwick legacy will prove as happy a store of memories as mine. From one generation to another . . ."

Rae is yet another of those who are repaying any debt they may think they owe for personal success by conducting a course on playwriting, giving a talk, or leading a discussion group. And it would appear that her wish for her son is being fulfilled for, in 1981, it was he who conducted the One-Act Play course.

Another account from one of those who feel that Swanwick can and does contribute greatly to their working lives must, I feel, be recorded here in full. Vivian Stuart writes: "I first attended the Writers' Summer School in 1952, a nervous beginner, with one published serial my whole claim to a serious interest in writing. Looking back, in 1982, with the completion of my 76th novel in sight, I can truthfully say that, had it not been for the School, I might never have become a full-time professional novelist. The friends I made that first magical year – many of them are still my friends – helped me to get my first novel published and set me on my way. I haven't missed a year since; the School is my annual stimulus, and, in gratitude for what it has given me in the past, I have tried to repay my debt by sharing my knowledge of trends and markets with those who come, for the first time, to learn how they, too, can become writers.

"The School gave me a number of 'firsts'. I was the first member of the School to be invited as a Speaker and I can still recall the trepidation with which I mounted the platform, clutching my speech in a trembling hand. My Chairman, who was John Boland, with the kindness for which he was renowned, gave me support. It was his hand that held me upright, when my knees threatened to buckle under me. And then the smiling, friendly faces and the warm applause – which make our School the best audience in the whole wide world – did the rest. I delivered my lecture with a confidence I had never had before and have never been afraid of speaking in public since. . . .

"I became the School's first woman Chairman by the narrow margin of two votes after a recount. I served in all for six years as Chairman. My other responsibilities at the School have been widely varied, ranging from being a first-aider to acting as doorperson. . . . I love the opportunity this gives me to greet new friends and old at the door of the Conference Hall and hear them say: 'Isn't Swanwick wonderful?' because it is. And I love my new 'label' – 'The only Bestselling Doorperson'."

These members, and many others with similar experience, are largely responsible for the continuing success of the School, for they are loyal to the organisation which has done so much for them and are eager that others shall share in that experience. Those who see the School from the outside, or who come for the first time, are frankly amazed at the way in which successful writers pass on information on markets, techniques and advice, to those who may well become their competitors. Leaders of courses and discussion groups are, in the main, drawn from the ever-growing number of members who owe their success to the School.

Then, of course, there are the lecturers. At the end of this book is a list of those who have served us in this way throughout the thirty-four years of our existence. It is an impressive list. They come without a fee – if they were paid adequately for their valuable contributions fees for members attending the School would rise to astronomical figures. Speakers are offered first-class travelling expenses, hospitality at The Hayes for themselves and their spouses or partners for as many of the six days as they wish to accept, which includes drinks and cigarettes and the freedom of Room X, the committee room, and also to have their books on sale in the Book Room. Many who accept the invitation for two or three days ask if they may extend their visit, while some return in other years as fee-paying members. It needs little imagination to realise how valuable they are. Jean Stubbs and Tony Corley are two whose names spring to mind in this connection and who cheerfully take courses and/or discussion groups or serve on panels.

Lecturers each give one lecture – followed by sustained questioning and discussion – and frequently take part in other discussions during the week. Most important, they circulate among the members as time and energy permit, making themselves available for personal and individual advice wherever and whenever possible. Their services are invaluable, and if there are times when they are not around they may be assisting at a small group meeting, talking professionally with an individual member, or even taking time off to relax, for Swanwick is not only stimulating, it can be demanding and exhausting.

What, then, have they talked about over the years which has been so productive for other writers? What a book would result if the lectures given at the different Schools were collected and published! Three hundred and forty lectures by some of the best known writers in this country and abroad! They have been well reported in trade papers such as *Smith's Trade News*, *John O' London's*, *The Writer*, *Freelance Writer and Photographer* – all, alas, now defunct – and *The Bookseller* has included features, while we have not gone unnoticed in the national and provincial newspapers and decidedly not on radio and television, from which media many of our lecturers have been drawn.

A few extracts from lectures given in those early days will give sufficient indication of the willingness of the successful writer to help the less successful.

A. E. Coppard, described as a teller of tales for all times and places and all sorts and conditions of readers, said, in a brilliant opening lecture: "The stuff of fiction, the food upon which the imagination has to feed and sustain itself, will be got from the common or uncommon matters of the world that is around us; the acts and beliefs of the people; their ambitions, desires, misfortunes, triumphs and, in particular, their conflicts.

"Having access to these things you will, if you have a first-class mind – and only then – obtain first-class results. No matter what quantity of material or variety of it that you may have access to, it will be of no avail to any

1949. Cecil Hunt and a group of Speakers at the first School.

class of mind unless it happens to be what we call a fictional mind: that is to say a mind that goes about noting people and events and conversations for the sinister purpose it has in view. A mind that, when it meets with a stimulating occasion, begins to effervesce and bubble over in extra-truthful amplification; a mind that is constantly conspiring with itself and contriving plots or bits of plots, and modifying or extending them as it thinks fit. In short, a mind of a liar, who desires to supplement truth in the interests of romance."

Then there was Marguerite Steen, novelist and playwright, who spoke one evening on *The Build-up of a Writer*. I remember her reaction as a black kitten found its way into the Conference Hall while she was speaking. This distinguished author of best-sellers, elegant in black evening skirt and white lace blouse, without interrupting herself, picked up the kitten and hugged it to her for the remainder of her lecture! If that action had not endeared her to her audience her lecture must have done. Beginner writers must have been encouraged when she said: "There is no such thing as a born writer. He is made – his life and his reactions to life make him. No experience is too trivial to be unimportant. To know people is more important than to know places, about which you can learn from libraries.

"One of the tests of the writer is complete indifference to whether seventy-five per cent of what he writes ever achieves publication. It should be regarded as exercises. I wrote and destroyed two full-length novels before it occurred to me that I might stand a chance of getting the third published.

"If you are a real writer, nothing can do you harm but a conflicting interest. If you can keep your bread-and-butter job in its place, strictly as a handmaid to your writing, it is all right. Journalism is too close as a bread-and-butter job, but a little journalism gives discipline, which is not a bad thing.

"There is a wide difference between education and culture, and the aspiring writer's first task is to bridge that gulf, to get out and acquire culture."

And then the tailpiece: "Self-criticism is vital, but it is one quality that seems to be left out of the make-up of most aspiring writers today."

Hard words but true.

Another thing that impressed me about Marguerite Steen at the time was that when, on her arrival at Swanwick, Sydney Goldsack presented her with a copy of her new book which Collins had just published, this so well-known author was as excited to see it as any of us might have been over our first published book. The title of that book was *Twilight on the Floods*.

Noel Streatfeild, well-known novelist and popular author of books for children, winner of the Carnegie Medal ten years before the first Summer School, described her method of work: "I get a family and make a chart with full details about everyone, including their birthdays and ages. After about three months I launch them into the career they are going to follow. It usually takes another three months to get to know the new world through children's eyes. I write about one children's book in two years." Condemning books of violence Noel Streatfeild said: "We've got it in our hands to give something better than violence, which is rotting the country away." She added, amid laughter – "Fill your house with books you want children to read and then say they are not to read them!"

Trevor Allen, novelist, biographer, reviewer, contributor to most of the leading newspapers and magazines, in his lecture on *One Man's Luck – The Adventures of a Freelance*, gave some sound advice to tyros, confirming what Marguerite Steen had said: "A reporting job is the finest experience any writer can have. It gets you into the habit of getting quickly off the mark. But," he advised, "don't keep it up too long. A few years is sufficient if you want to do general freelancing. I hardly read a paper without taking and indexing cuttings for my file. Get an expert to check your articles if they are on technical subjects and always send a copy of any interview to the person concerned. It is more sensible to be a good journalist than a bad or indifferent novelist."

He also spoke about the importance of amending the article or other piece of writing to suit the editor, who usually has good reason for wishing it to be done.

Helena Grose, one of Collins' romantic novelists, also endorsed what other lecturers had said to beginner writers. Her subject was *The Motives Behind the (Would-be) Best Seller*.

"Don't be content to learn of life through books and films and the radio," she said. "These will never feed your gift. Aim at self-development through first-hand experience and new social contacts. A theme is not necessary to your story but it gives it depth and acts as a scaffold. You must plot your story. Plot the actual incidents in settings suitable to develop your story."

It is not surprising that much was addressed to beginner writers, for the School was started with them particularly in mind, but the mixtures proved to be adequate for all tastes and forms of writing.

John Benn spoke about *Publishing and Technical Writing* and Sydney Goldsack chipped in with comments from his experience as a director of Collins. We were reminded by John Brophy of the reviewers' and readers' parts in evaluating our work and making it known, while on another afternoon John Moore gave us a personal anthology, transporting us to the Cotswolds in his talk about his country books. With Cynthia Pughe we studied the technique of radio drama, concluding the week on the last morning with a lecture by Edgar Osborne, County Librarian of the Derbyshire County Libraries, his subject being *The Author and the Public Library*.

This was the pattern set by first-year lecturers. The week was drawing to a close but there were still the winding-up events to come and, most important, the Business Meeting to discuss the value of the week and decide on the future.

8

Day of Decision

The last day of that first memorable Summer School had come. Early the next morning the great exodus would take place.

Many were the regrets expressed from breakfast-time onwards that the School was drawing to a close, with its stimulation, inspiration and companionship. The exhaustion following a period of such intense activity would not be felt until later. Now was the time to take stock and look ahead; to make plans to put to good use what had been gained during these unique days.

Everyone seemed anxious to squeeze the most out of these last lectures and discussion groups. But would there be another School? If so, where would it be held? These were the questions on most lips when we assembled in a crowded conference hall for the First Annual General Meeting.

In a fever of anxiety, and with the full knowledge of the Chairman, I sought an interview with the Manager, Wally Milne, in his office before the meeting started. I remember well the questions asked and answered.

"If we decide to have a School another year I very much doubt whether our members will agree to come here," I began.

"Why not?" asked Wally, though he well knew what my answer would be.

"The bedroom and bathroom accommodation is too Spartan and the washing facilities are communal," I replied. "There's too much stodgy food, and the meat is tough."

"That's why it costs you so little. Most of our clients want to keep the price down, but if you care to pay more I can improve the quality of the food. As for the rest, I intend to plough the profits back into the place. It's not yet recovered from the effects of the war, you know, but if you can persuade your members to come here and pay a little extra I promise you there will be improvements each year."

With that assurance I asked for a tentative date for the next year and was offered one in September, August being fully booked.

"Too late for our school-teachers," I protested.

"If that's so, I'll see what I can do to make adjustments," said the ever-helpful Wally. And he did.

Now we wear green and white name labels – white for those attending for the first time and green for the others. Those with white labels may attend and take part at the Business Meeting, but have no voting rights. In 1949 there was no such distinction – we were all founder members and, as such, entitled to vote.

After the Secretary's Report and the financial statement had been presented and approved, the Chairman rose to ask: "Is it your wish that we have a Summer School next year?"

A forest of hands went up while voices thundered – "Yes!"

This, in itself, was tribute enough but, as one member reported, many were the calls for votes of thanks, and many were the expressions of gratitude to those who had worked so hard to make the School such a success.

There was, as anticipated, some discussion about the venue, some members thinking we could do better, but when the financial position was explained, together with the Manager's promise of improvements, the vote in favour of Swanwick was almost unanimous. And how wise that decision was. To the best of my knowledge there has been no need to raise the question of venue since. Swanwick has become the home of the Writers' Summer School.

Earlier in the week, following Marguerite Steen's lecture, Sydney Goldsack made a spontaneous presentation of a gold pen and pencil set to the Secretary on behalf of those present, as a token of appreciation of the part she had played in organising the School. Cecil Hunt, that so popular Chairman, was visibly affected when – presented with a brief-case – he realised exactly how much he meant to all the members.

He had endeared himself to all and the prolonged and enthusiastic applause which greeted his acceptance of chairing the 1950 School was deafening. There was a unanimous vote that the existing secretary be re-elected Secretary/Treasurer, thus combining the duties of both offices. The selection of the committee was left to the discretion of the Chairman and Secretary. We decided to keep it small in number partly to save expense and also because of the greater ease in arranging meetings. Harold Harris, Managing Editor of *The Writer*, who had done so much to publicise the first School, agreed to join us, as did Mary Dunn, a Glasgow member who was to have her first serial published in *Woman's Weekly* while she was at the School.

The day finished with a grand concert and social, followed by dancing until the small hours of the morning. I think it was at the first School that some wit (and I don't know who it was) wrote and produced what came to be known as the Swanwick Song which we all sang with gusto. This continued to be sung on the last night of each School until about 1970. It was set to a popular tune and a small choir was drawn from the members to lead the singing, the accompaniment being vigorously played by Lilian Cullup, then our excellent pianist and organist. Jill Dick has sent me a copy of the song:

> "Some people go to Butlins
> And live in little huts,
> But we all come to Swanwick
> Why? because we're slightly nuts.

We learn to write best-sellers
In the Conference Hall
But the tales you hear by the old duck pond
You remember best of all."

Early the next morning the great exodus began, with coaches drawn up in front of the house ready to take rail passengers away first. When they had departed, after many farewells and promises to meet again at Swanwick in 1950, the drivers of the three London coaches began handling the luggage belonging to their passengers. Meanwhile those members travelling by car were making their departure. When some two hundred and fifty people all depart from one centre within an hour or so it is hardly surprising that every year some luggage is overlooked and only discovered when there is a frantic telephone call from a station or stopping place, but I have never yet heard of its not reaching its rightful owner by some means or other.

And so the first School ended, but plans were already being made for the next.

Departure Day. Marjorie Harris, third from left.

"If nothing succeeds like success," wrote Hugh Stephens, at the end of his account in *The Freelance Writer and Photographer*, "our week at The Hayes, Swanwick, next year should qualify for Hollywood superlatives. Come!"

And come they did at the end of August – all two hundred and sixty, more than half that number being drawn in by the tales they heard about that first Swanwick Summer School for Writers.

9

The Same High Standard

To record the first thirty-four years of our existence one by one would be both tedious and invidious, for the pattern was not a changing but a continuing one. For this reason I propose, in this second part of our history, simply to fill in the gaps, highlight special events, reveal some of the results, quoting from the reports received from some who have attended over the years, and, if space permits, quote further snippets from lectures and from the media.

One interesting point not mentioned so far is the religious content of the School. The Constitution drawn up in 1956 (about which more later) specifically rules that the organisation shall be *non-religious*, although I think *non-sectarian* would be more apt. This was inserted to avoid discussions developing into arguments on theological and sectarian questions about which there might be such strong divergence of opinion that it would profit no one and destroy the happy atmosphere which is so evident. However, with a chapel built in the grounds in which it is customary for the management to arrange for a Sunday morning service – the different conferences often, but not of necessity, supplying the preacher or leader and providing the organist – we have always planned our programmes to leave a free period on Sunday morning so that members who wish may attend the service without missing any session. It is pleasing to see the Chapel so crowded for that service, every seat usually being occupied. On Sunday mornings some breakfast tables are kept free for those who arrive late after attending early morning service in the village.

From the very early years there has been a request for a "Lift Up Your Hearts" service in the Chapel each morning before breakfast, with different members of the School leading the devotions, and this has continued to be well supported. Yet another request from members was for a discussion group on *Writing for the Religious Press* and each year these discussions have been a regular part of the programme.

While on the subject of religion it is interesting to recall that, in 1972, the B.B.C. came to record an "Any Questions" programme for Radio 4 on *Questions of Belief*. Jack Singleton (who organised many competitions on radio for scholarships to the Writers' Summer School) was the producer, and Geoffrey Smith, leader writer of *The Times*, chaired the session. The panel consisted of Mary Stott, Woman's Editor of *The Guardian*, and a speaker at the School that year; Edward Blishen, novelist, editor, critic and educationist; and John Ferguson, Dean of the Faculty of Arts at the Open University and Chairman of the Education Committee of the British Council of Churches. Members of the School asked the questions, which were on religious, moral and social issues. The programme was broadcast on Sunday evening, 17th September, that year.

I still have a letter from Cecil Hunt in which he said that he thought the programme for the 1950 School needed a "little less congestion" than that which we planned for the first event, when we invited twelve lecturers. In 1950, therefore, we reduced the number of lecturers to ten, replacing the second session in the morning either with discussion groups or courses, and this has been the pattern ever since. Even so, this has made little difference to the number of sessions crowded into those six days for, once caught up in the atmosphere, the desire to gain the maximum benefit from each School led to so much pressure being exerted by members for more and more discussion groups on more and more aspects of writing, that the days appear to be as fully occupied as it is possible to make them, with sessions of one kind or another continuing until 11 p.m. on most evenings. The fact that attendance is optional makes no difference, for rooms in which these take place are often overcrowded.

Geoffrey Lamb, a schoolmaster who retired early to do full-time writing, and who has now had over seventy books published, sums up his impressions: "Twenty-seven years ago there was only an informal 'get-together' on the first evening, which seemed to consist in everyone except me getting together with everybody else. Perhaps I'm rather slow at making friends. But by the afternoon of the second day things had changed. I had met one or two kindred spirits, and was quickly swept up in the swirl of Swanwick activity.

"Since then I have attended sixteen or eighteen times, and heard approximately one hundred and eight lectures and joined over a hundred discussion groups. A few of the latter I've conducted myself. I've also made some valued friendships.

"Over the years I've enjoyed almost all the talks. But the special thing about Swanwick is not just the lectures but the combination of talks, discussions (formal and informal), dancing, tea on the lawn, coffee in the lounge, table tennis in the Vinery, congestion in the bookshop, pandemonium in the dining-room, and a dozen other items."

One of the remarks made to Cecil Hunt at the second School had a profound effect on my future. Towards the end of that second experience of Swanwick, Cecil said to me: "Frank Knight, one of your Croydon members, has just said: 'Nancy will never finish her book for Macmillans while she remains Secretary of the Summer School.'"

My response came quickly, without the need of further thought. "Frank is right. You'll have to find another Secretary. I'm determined to get on Macmillan's list." I did finish the book and went on to write for that publisher for the next twenty-five years.

But Cecil seemed a little concerned at first, although he appreciated the reason for my decision, for he knew how much work was involved in the organisation of the School. The main problem was to find someone not quite so involved with writing yet wholly committed to the School and its ideals. Eileen Jackson, whom we had never met and who was not a member of the School but who was the principal of a secretarial agency and the sister of one of the members present at the Annual General Meeting, agreed to become Secretary/ Treasurer for the following year, and was duly appointed.

I was appointed Speakers' Secretary and it was my task to cover all communications with lecturers.

That was the time when there was a strong request from parents for the next School to be held in July, prior to the school holidays. The date was accordingly fixed for 2nd to 8th July.

The change of date was unfortunate, for membership of the School that year reached only 140 as against 251 the previous year, which not only made a considerable difference to receipts but resulted in our not reaching the guaranteed number of 200 members attending. The balance of receipts against expenditure was so small that it was insufficient to meet the amount due to The Hayes under the guarantee. While Mr. Milne generously offered to waive the guarantee if we made a booking for the next year, there would still be no balance to carry forward to start the School of 1952. There was considerable alarm when the financial situation was revealed but, in spite of this, there was a unanimous vote in favour of the School being held in 1952. The financial situation was fully discussed, resulting in a resolution being passed unanimously that members be invited to donate such sums of money as they felt able to afford to ensure a guarantee for next year; these sums to be refunded should the School pay for itself, which would happen if the full number attended. A further resolution that members of the School be asked to make a minimum contribution of 10s.0d as a gift, was also carried unanimously.

Thus the financial position of the School was secured for another year. Due to the generosity of the management of The Hayes in waiving the guarantee a balance of approximately £50 on the present year's working could be anticipated, and £35.17s.0d. was received in gifts from members, with loans finally reaching £166.14s.0d.

John Boland had been a member of each School and was, in fact, a delegate from Birmingham Writers' Group at the inaugural meeting at the Institute of Journalists in 1948. I have never understood why he was not then recognised as being a potentially good and useful member of the organising committee. We could well have used his services in those days but, in fact, he did not join the committee until 1953, although he attended every year prior to that. He always arrived early and made himself available to assist with luggage and help show members to their rooms as they arrived. Philippa did not come with him the first year – they had only been married a few months before the first School started and John was at the beginning of his writing career. Also Philippa had not then given up her job as a photographer's assistant and first came in 1950 as the photographer's assistant, for in those early years we always had an official photographer at the school. By the following year (1951) Philippa had given up her job and has been very actively employed at each School since then.

It was John who led the way in solving the financial problem at that July School, for it was he who first suggested that members should make loans to put the School's finances in order. In his forthright way he marched boldly forward to the platform and placed a five-pound note in an ash tray on the table. Immediately others followed with the result already stated.

If anything was needed to assess the value of the school to those present, and their determination that it should continue, this episode certainly made it clear.

Dianne Doubtfire, who was attending for the first time, wrote afterwards: "I was lucky enough to attend the third Summer School and I can remember my excitement when I danced with Cecil Hunt at the gala dance with the live band and sumptuous buffet supper. I was thirty-two and had published nothing but a few poems (unpaid-for). When we were asked for contributions to ensure the continuation of the School I had no money of my own but gave three pounds out of the housekeeping. I felt I would gladly have pawned all my possessions to help! Everyone must have felt the same enthusiasm because donations poured in from all sides. We knew we must be prepared to lose our money if the venture failed but of course we had it returned the following year.

"I feel I owe everything to the School. Without those marvellous lectures and discussion groups, and the unstinted advice I received year after year from so many generous and warm-hearted people, I could never have succeeded so soon, if at all. I'm tremendously grateful to those who worked so hard to launch the School and all who keep it going so magnificently."

10

Changes in Personnel

It was at that same General Meeting, when the School's future was in such jeopardy, that we suffered another shattering blow. Our popular and efficient chairman, Cecil Hunt, anounced that he could not accept chairmanship of the School for another year. Efforts were made to persuade him but to no purpose. Those who knew him best were aware that, although he had been only too willing to get the School started, he must have been under considerable strain from a health point of view.

However, he told the members that Garry Hogg had agreed to take over as Chairman if the School so wished and Beth Hogg (Elizabeth Grey) was willing to act as Secretary/Treasurer. They had been at Swanwick in 1950 when Garry had given the opening lecture and were now Host and Hostess, Garry also serving as Vice-Chairman. Strong pressure was put on Cecil and Kathleen Hunt to become Host and Hostess of the 1952 School but Cecil had a very firm conviction that it was better for him to keep away from the School for a year or two. Doubtless he was right but he did, later, accept an invitation to be a lecturer at the 1954 School and we were all eagerly anticipating his return. His name was included on the programme among the other lecturers for that year, his subject being *The Short Story*.

The School was due to commence on 14th August that year and on 13th July we heard the shattering news that Cecil Hunt had suddenly collapsed and died that day. He was fifty-one.

His biographical notes as recorded in the programme for that year are worth noting here; they reveal his literary qualities and experience: "Former literary agent, former literary editor of the *Daily Mail* and Fiction Editor of the *Evening News*. Author of many books including *Ink in my Veins* (autobiography), several collections of *Schoolboy Howlers*, *A Dictionary of Word-Makers*, *Living by the Pen*, *Short Stories: How to Write Them*, etc. Contributor of short stories to many periodicals. First Chairman of the Writers' Summer School."

He had forty books published – no mean achievement in a life of only fifty-one years and with all his other commitments. He was indeed a very hard worker and was never happier than when working or helping other writers. He gave himself whole-heartedly to the school while in office. He could have added to his other credentials that he was much in demand as a lecturer, being on Foyle's Lecture Agency's list of speakers. In spite of that he did not hesitate to accept engagements to speak at Writers' Circles in different parts of the country as opportunity offered. To the best of my knowledge he charged no fee when speaking to writers. He was a very good literary agent and gave me much good advice on my first two books for Macmillan. Two of our Croydon Writers' Circle members used him as their agent and he placed their first and subsequent books with publishers until his untimely death. They thought very highly of his criticism and ability as an agent and both became professional writers, one of them winning the Carnegie Medal with a book placed by Cecil with Faber & Faber. He was Chairman of London Writer Circle for many years and became President for the last two or three years of his life. He had a great sense of humour.

Cecil's widow, Kathleen Hunt, lives in Dorset and we correspond once or twice a year. She wrote recently sending me some cuttings and photographs relating to the early years at Swanwick and wishing this book every success. She added: "I have no particular memories of Cecil's thoughts about the School except that he was full of enthusiasm for the whole idea (he was always keen to help the budding writer) and he was very much looking forward to being a lecturer in 1954."

At the business meeting at that School the question of a memorial to Cecil Hunt was discussed and it was decided that the most fitting tribute would be to institute a scholarship of a free place at the Writers' Summer School each year to be known as the Cecil Hunt Scholarship and this has been awarded each year since his death. The first competition for this was organised by *John O'London's*, a well-known literary magazine at that time, long since defunct, after which the B.B.C. organised it through some of their programmes but eventually had to discontinue this because the task became too onerous, as many as 5,000 entries being received one year when Jack Singleton was running this! It is now organised through the medium of *Competitor's Journal*.

Other scholarships have been awarded by friends of the School. John Gordon awarded one when he opened the School in 1959, as did Jean Plaidy when she was first lecturer and then hostess. Iris Harvey, a Derby supporter, awarded one in the early years, investing a sum of money with the School so that it could be awarded each year. This is still organised by a provincial paper. When Vivian Stuart started the Romantic Novelists' Association a free place at the Summer School was awarded by that Association for the best novel in that field.

Up to and including 1955 the School had continued as it had started, with no definite Constitution, but at the Annual General Meeting that year Muriel Goaman (Bideford) proposed that a Constitution be drawn up especially in relation to the election of future officers of the School. The motion was seconded by Kay Blundell the School's auditor. It was agreed that it should be left for discussion by the 1956 committee who duly considered it, with the result that a document was circulated to all members with the programme for that year. At the Annual General Meeting it was put before the members and agreed unanimously. Various amendments have been adopted since that time.

Alan Wykes was Chairman that year, John Boland was Vice-Chairman and I and my husband, Leslie Salmon, were Secretary and Treasurer, with Kay Blundell and Bill Lowndes on the Committee. We were the team which formulated the draft Constitution.

The Constitution states that "With the exception of the Secretary and Treasurer, no officer or committee member shall serve for more than three consecutive years, but after the lapse of one year shall be eligible for re-electing". However, in 1980 the Committee decided that the School should be asked to consider the resolution that "The three year rule be suspended in Michael Legat's particular case to enable him to stand again for election as Chairman of the 1981 School," the nomination to be made by the Committee. Michael had previously lectured at Swanwick on three occasions and had been a particularly successful Chairman during his three years in that office. Several of us felt that it was important to retain his close interest in the School and to ensure that his abilities were used to the best advantage.

I was deputed, as an Honorary Life Member, to explain the situation to the members at the Welcome Meeting of that School and to ask them to endorse the proposal. They did so by an overwhelming majority and the nomination was therefore put forward at the Annual General Meeting. There were no other nominations, but a somewhat heated debate took place before Michael was elected for a fourth consecutive year. I should make it clear that most of the comparatively few members who opposed his re-election were at pains to explain that they did not do so on personal grounds but because they felt it wrong to go against the Constitution. My own feeling is that, important though adherence to the Constitution may be, there are times when it may seem too rigid and a bending of the rules may be to the benefit of the School.

It was in 1954, when the School had recovered from its earlier financial setbacks and numbers attending had reached a viable figure, that there was a move to limit the registrations to a level which would result in receipts being only a little higher than adequate to meet expenses, the idea apparently being that this would make for "greater friendliness" and the easier accessibility to speakers and course and discussion group leaders. Yet there was increasing accommodation available at The Hayes because of the additional bedrooms and other facilities being built under Wally's improvement plan. I find it difficult to understand the reasoning behind this in the light of the very many letters received which referred to the friendliness experienced being such a feature of the School. I imagine it would almost cause a riot if, at the present time, places were limited below the potential of the accommodation when there is such dismay among those who cannot get a place even though registering and sending full fees more than six months before the date of the School, and with accommodation available for more than 350. Not one letter I have received or one remark I have heard suggests the School suffers from increasing numbers attending, or that there is any less friendliness than formerly.

The practice of sending full fees in February has existed ever since competition for places has been so keen, preference being given to such applicants. Interest from the investment of the money enables the fees charged to members to be kept to a very reasonable figure and also covers the cost of the scholarships which the School funds.

As evidence that the Summer School was maintaining its earlier reputation I quote from a letter received from Monica Ewer in 1957 after her husband and she had been Host and Hostess that year:

"Trilby, who is a fairly cynical bloke, came away

enormously impressed, feeling that the School was serving a really useful purpose, filling a want, and that he would like to help it along if the opportunity ever came." (It did, we asked him back as lecturer; he was diplomatic correspondent of the *Daily Herald*.) "It isn't often he feels like that," added Monica. "In a way a week like that restores one's belief in people – everyone so kind and so pleased with the simple things of life. I loved to hear their chatter and the only sad aspect is that one feels so many must be lonely the rest of the year. And I worry, too, about their high hopes when we all know the disappointment inevitable in our profession.

"If at any time I can help you be sure to let me know."

An additional clause (22) was added to the Constitution in 1957. It reads: "The School may, by a resolution of an Annual General Meeting, passed by not less than two-thirds of those full members present and voting, confer an honorary life-membership upon certain persons who by long and faithful service have contributed materially to the furtherance and success of the School, providing such persons shall be founder members and have served the School in an official capacity for not less than three years. (The definition of a founder member being one who was present at the meeting held on the 11th June 1948, when by a unanimous vote of those present the Writers' Summer School was officially founded.)"

At the Annual General Meeting in 1961 John Boland and I had honorary life-membership conferred on us, while, in 1977, Marjorie Harris was also given that honour.

Obviously, over a period of thirty-four years, many of our members must have died. Some we hear about but some we do not. Of those we do know some have served as officers. First, in January 1966, my husband, Leslie Salmon, died unexpectedly after a short illness. Although for years he had suffered from Parkinson's disease he had been a regular supporter of the School

John Boland with Lettice Cooper.

A. A. Thomson at the wicket.

Leonora Starr.

Ursula Bloom and her husband.

from the time of the first formal committee meeting held at our house in Shirley, and was always at hand to do whatever was required. Without his help I could not have coped with the work of organising those early schools.

Then, on 15th August, 1969, during the evening prior to the opening of the School for its 21st Anniversary, Maurice Symons died. He had been our Treasurer since 1965 and had been suffering from ill health for a few weeks prior to the opening date of the School. He had sent a written report clearly showing the financial position of the School. He concluded his report as follows: "I must end this report on a part sad, part glad note. Sad that my present illness prevents me continuing to act as your Treasurer; glad to be able to say 'It's all been great fun while it lasted,' and glad, too, to say, 'Thank you, Marjorie Harris, for five years amiable co-operation in the administration of the Writers' Summer School.'"

Maurice and his wife, Joan, had endeared themselves to all by their quiet, unassuming manner and the obvious desire they both had to help the School to run smoothly and efficiently. Our very deep sympathy was expressed with the widow and it was agreed that she be offered a free place at Swanwick the next year, an offer which she graciously accepted. At the Annual General Meeting in 1973 Joan Symons was elected Treasurer, an office which she has most worthily held up to and including the present time.

Then, on 9th November 1976, we suffered a grievous loss by the death of John Boland, one of our Honorary Life Members who had been such a stalwart supporter of the School since its inauguration in 1948. He was Chairman for three years, from 1958 to 1960 inclusive, and from 1973 to 1975 inclusive served with me as Joint Chairman, and had also been Vice-Chairman and a Lecturer and had served as a committee member for many years, becoming Host with Philippa, a delightful Hostess, for seven years.

His death left a big gap, but it was a tribute to both him and his wife that Philippa continued as Hostess from 1973 to 1982, when she was appointed Secretary of the 1983 School following the resignation of Marjorie Harris from that office.

At the Annual General Meeting in 1978 a resolution was passed that "Philippa Boland be made an Honorary Member of the School, with a continuous invitation to attend it, in view of the long and faithful service she has given to the School for the past twenty-five years, mostly in an official capacity, as the wife of a former Life Member".

In 1977 we lost by death another tried and trusted committee member when Albert Rhodes died only a matter of months after John Boland's death. Albert and Eileen were to have been Host and Hostess to the Members that year, an office which was created for a short time, and in that case also, Eileen agreed to hold that office with another member of the School in place of her husband.

There is space to mention only one other member whose death was a sad loss to the School. Philip King had been attending as a fee-paying member for very many years and, although never parading his popularity and great success as a playwright, became a friend to all with whom he came in contact. He was persuaded to serve on the committee in 1973 and 1974 but would not accept any other office, although he did give one lecture and conduct a course on playwriting. Many could quote stories about him and his quiet, unobtrusive advice which was available for all who asked for or needed it, but I quote from a tribute sent to me by Marjorie Wing, of Leicester, who first attended the School in 1960 and has, I believe, been every year since. She writes: "Before his lecture in 1968, on *Writing for the Theatre*, he suffered from stage fright! But nerves vanished as he spoke in his glorious resonant voice, telling of his adventures in theatre street. The rafters rang with our mirth as Philip King unfurled the story of his career.

"Albert Rhodes, a playwright himself, told me that during Philip's first year, he found himself sitting next to him at breakfast. Noting that on Philip's white label he had written 'Playwriting', Albert asked: 'Have you written any plays?' 'A few,' replied Philip. Albert, trying to make a white label feel at home, then asked: 'Any published?' 'Yes,' said Philip. 'What was it?' enquired Albert. Casually Philip replied, '*See How They Run.*' 'That was when I dropped my coffee cup,' Albert told me.

"Swanwick became a yearly event for Philip. A highlight of our leisure time at the School was when we could get Philip talking. I remember on one occasion five of us didn't even change or wash before dinner, we were so engrossed in his anecdotes and could not break up the party.

"On the Sunday before his death, when we had just received our registration forms, I telephoned him. Diffidently I asked if he would make it this year. For a moment weakness was forgotten as he said, in those resonant tones, 'Of course I will. I shall see you all at The Hayes.' Those were the last words I heard him speak. His well-loved presence has left an impression on the Writers' Summer School that will not fade away."

11

Landmarks

In 1969 we celebrated the twenty-first anniversary of the Writers' Summer School, the main event being a special dinner with Sir Robert Lusty, Managing Director of Hutchinson's, as Guest of Honour. Mr. and Mrs. Milne also accepted an invitation to join us at dinner. Ruth Martin's article in the trade press about the event carried the headline BIGGEST EVER ATTENDANCE AT WRITERS' SUMMER SCHOOL. Attendance that year reached 338.

In proposing the toast of 'The School' Sir Robert reminded the members that Hutchinsons had been involved with the School from the beginning, Harold Harris, the Managing Editor of *The Writer* (to whom reference has already been made), having attended the first two schools.

John Boland replied to the toast on behalf of the School and I was given the privilege of proposing a toast to The Hayes, to which Wally Milne replied in his usual witty style. Later a gift of books and a pen were presented to Mr. and Mrs. Milne as a token of their work for the School over the past twenty-one years.

The evening concluded with a party in the Conference Hall at which eight members who had attended the first school in 1949 were presented with special badges.

During the course of the week a television camera crew filmed various sessions in action for the Midland "Today" programme.

In 1973 we celebrated the twenty-fifth anniversary, when John Boland and I were Joint Chairmen and proposed the toasts at the special dinner.

Writing about this anniversary in *Trade News*, Ruth Martin gave a résumé of how the School was founded and how it developed over the years. In her opening paragraph she wrote: "No less than 340 writers attended. . . . If you imagine this is just a large bunch of dilettantes or would-be scribblers assembling for a pleasant week's holiday, forget it. The work-load is enormous, and the dedication well-nigh unbelievable.

"This year the weather was fabulous, but whilst the meetings were in session few indeed were those who ducked out and sought a shady spot under the trees or down by the little lake. The great majority had come to listen, learn and contribute, and no amount of hot, brilliant sunshine was going to deter them. I never fail to be astonished at the generosity with which people pass on ideas . . . and advice to others. . . . I'd not been back to Swanwick for four years, but I found the generosity as prevalent as ever. It's what goes to make up the indefinable 'spirit of Swanwick'."

In 1978 the thirtieth anniversary was marked with the presentation to every member of a bookmark, and at dinner one evening a glass of wine was provided and the School's health was drunk.

But of course there have been criticisms, although surprisingly few considering the size of the School and the length of time it has existed. For example, in 1965 a long and well-reasoned article appeared in *Books and Bookmen* under the title "What's Wrong with the Summer School?" Many of the points raised had, of course, been discussed and considered frequently over the years by those who care most about the School and its values because they have given up an enormous amount of time to its organisation, and have been happy to do so, knowing, from first-hand evidence, its value to a very great number of writers. The fact that it is still increasing in numbers, with letters telling of stimulation and *inspiration* gained, and of writing more successfully, does show that there is not much wrong with the Writers' Summer School.

In any case, the School is organised democratically and all members have the opportunity at the Annual General Meeting of airing and discussing any changes they think necessary, when a vote can be taken and the whole School decide whether any action needs to be taken.

In 1979 *The Bookseller* commissioned Ruth Martin to write a long article on the Writers' Summer School, in the course of which she recorded that, in addition to the main lectures that year, there were eight courses of three sessions each, fifteen talks, twenty discussion groups and four panels, on which several of the main speakers served. Of the 340 members attending fifteen were from overseas – including visitors from New Zealand, Nigeria, Canada and America. Many other applications had to be turned down, including forty-five from America alone.

She added – "It was Ronald Whiting's first visit to Swanwick and he expressed himself as being surprised and delighted at its range. One of the things which impressed him most was the amazing generosity with which people were prepared to pass on useful information of every kind, and the willingness of successful writers to help those still endeavouring to get published."

How glad Cecil Hunt would have been to know that this generosity so constantly referred to had become such a characteristic of Swanwick, for this was the reason for proposing the School in the first place – he wanted the successful to help the less successful.

Michael Legat is recorded as saying:

"When I first came to Swanwick in 1964 I saw it as a gathering of rather frustrated writers who would never get published anyway. I couldn't have been more wrong. A very large number of people were already successful to some extent, and were here to learn more about their particular craft. But above all, and this is what I believe makes Swanwick work – writing is a very lonely business (a good old cliché but it's true) and this is one week in the year when everybody shares your interest and your problems. This, I think, is what generates the tremendous enthusiasm and which keeps the Writers' Summer School going.'

It is obvious the members are aware of this. Take Margaret Thomson Davis as an example. In her book – *The Making of a Novelist* – she writes: "I'd had a great many short stories published. My real goal in life, however, had always been to become a novelist. . . . Now I was able to spur myself on by repeating to myself that if I could get short work into print, I could get long work into print. It was just a matter of sticking at it and learning the appropriate techniques.

"With this in mind I travelled down to Derbyshire to attend my first Writers' Summer School. This is where I met my dear wee friend John Maloney. I can still see him hirping about excitedly (he had a club foot) among all the writers in that beautiful place. I was overcome with hysterical excitement myself. Here, at last, I was among my own kind. Here were writers – three hundred of them – all bursting to talk about writing. Gloriously happy times! I've gone every year since with the same deliriously happy excitement and I have left at the end of the week . . . so many dearly-loved friends.

"That first year one of the lecturers was Alex Cordell. . . . Later, outside on the sunny lawn – I plucked up courage to approach Cordell. I spilled out all my troubles (everyone does this to everyone else all the time at Swanwick) of how I'd written five novels and none of them were any use and how I desperately wanted to write books that would get published.

"True to what I now know to be the Swanwick tradition he gave me his help and advice in a most generous and unassuming way. . . . 'Go back from Swanwick,' he said, 'and sit down and, with as much courage and honesty as you can muster, write a book about Glasgow and about life in the Glasgow tenements.' I stared at him in astonishment. It had never occurred to me to do that. On my way home from Swanwick I closed my eyes and drifted back into the jungle of Glasgow streets. I eventually wrote a book called *The Prisoner*. . . ."

Margaret sent me some information about John Maloney, whom I well remember. He phoned Margaret just a few days before Swanwick and told her he was not feeling too well. He said: "If only I can keep all right so that I can get to Swanwick and see all my friends. . . ." That was all he worried about.

The next morning Margaret had a telephone call to say John had died the previous night. He was seated by the telephone, having just phoned her. He had no one to talk to about writing except his Swanwick friends, of whom Margaret was one. Swanwick was the most important thing in his life and gave him great happiness.

Angela Griffiths was another one-time lonely writer who first came to Swanwick in 1976. She writes: "If I did not write I felt restless and if I did write I felt vaguely discontented, knowing the finished product was not the creation I meant it to be, but a jumble of words, without shape. And then I discovered Swanwick and everything fell into place. It was happiness personified, a taste of bliss.

"Swanwick is much more than a Summer School for budding writers: it's a feeling, a fellowship, a 'happening' which is quite unlike anything outside its own boundaries. After being on the waiting list for several years running, my first visit was bound to be especially exciting. I remember arriving at the great house and feeling light-headed with joy at the thought of spending almost a week in such a beautiful setting with over three hundred like-minded souls. That first impression is still clear in my mind. Tea was being served on the sunlit terrace to the sound of happy chatter and laughter.

There was such a friendly, caring atmosphere, and the topic of every conversation seemed to be on one theme, writing. It was as though I had searched along the wavebands of a radio and suddenly found the right signal. Now I was with my own kind and the secret ambition to be an author no longer seemed such an impossible dream. The opportunity was within reach.

"I hoped it would be a short apprenticeship, but it took several years before I gained as much as a toe-hold on the first rung of the ladder. Then things gradually improved, thanks to successive Swanwick time, until 1982 when a fair number of works met with success. I still have a lot to learn and one good year does not make a knight of the plume!

"Swanwick taught me confidence and versatility. It also gave me friends. These are people I see once a year, but each time we meet it's as though we'd never left the Summer School."

Elizabeth Elgin, of Boroughbridge, North Yorkshire, came for the first time in 1969, the twenty-first anniversary year. She writes: "I drove Myra Taylor and Carla Lane down there. They had just 'made it'; a pilot play on television and a series to follow. They had created *The Liver Birds* and that year they were the darlings of Summer School.

"We stood apart, me and my white label, longing to be one of those wonderful people. It really hurt me, not being published; not knowing anything. By the end of that week I knew that absolutely nothing would prevent me from becoming a writer.

"I went around in a daze. I listened in on conversations. I was talked to and talked at. By the end of the week I was almost a part of it all. Hadn't I actually spoken to Catherine Cookson? And not just in passing, but half an hour together, she and I, and talking like equals.

"'I'm coming back,' I vowed. 'Next year I'll have a green label and I'll be published. This time next year I'll hold my head up at Summer School because I'll really belong.' And I did. During the year that followed I sold three articles and a short story. I had earned my green label and those four acceptances were only for starters. At Summer School 1970 I made another promise. By next year, I solemnly swore, I'd have a novel finished. And it was finished, and accepted too!

"So each year I set myself a target. Summer School is where I charge my batteries to see me through another year. Without it I'm lost. I know that, because one year I didn't get a place there. I won't ever forget it, nor will my family! 1975 – the year of the Waiting List!

"Summer Schoolers are wonderful people. They are happy for your successes; they buoy you up when you've had a rejection. You can pour out your innermost secrets to any one of them, and they won't tell. They'll give you their time, discuss the storyline of your next novel in detail with you, and not pinch one word of it.

"Summer Schoolers probably have their secret rituals, as I have. I like to arrive early and do a tour of The Hayes just to make sure that nothing has changed. Then I circuit the duck pond, and tell myself that I'm really here. I say a silent thank-you for nearly 200 short stories, five serials and nine novels. I vow to try to help someone who was once like myself; to give something back because Summer School has given so generously to me; taught me so much."

Frances Crowne, a member of Slough Writers' Circle, who has been coming to Swanwick since 1972, and is now a well-established writer helping others as she feels she has been helped by Summer School, writes: "From my first attendance ten years ago, Swanwick will always be the coach arriving at Derby station and seeing the late John Boland smilingly checking our names off his list. Later, Nancy Martin, Joan Symons, Marjorie Harris, Philippa Boland, Stanley Wilson, those lovely people with their happy welcome will ever remain special to me.

"All that, and home-made jam and bees too. The

sunshine and the garden at The Hayes. But perhaps, finally, it's the laughter and the friendships which remain long after we have ended our lovely, noisy week's occupation of Swanwick, and our writing can only be deeply enriched by the experience.''

And Pamela Pope, from Lymington, when sending me photographs she had taken of The Hole through which the prisoner got away, wrote: ''I can truthfully say that the Summer School has changed my life. I came for the first time in 1971 and was quite overcome. It was 1975 before I braved it again, having then had a lot of short stories published, mostly in confession magazines. I have now been seven times and in 1980 I attended the Romantic Fiction course run by Mary Wibberley. Mary was wonderful. She gave me an enthusiastic criticism of my first chapter of a romantic novel and insisted I should send it with a synopsis to Mills & Boon. This I did and it was accepted right away, the rest of the novel being asked for as soon as possible. It was the first novel I had ever written. It came out in hardback in February and in paperback in July. It is also a Harlequin paperback in America. My second book has been accepted and I have almost completed the third.

''I am not as quick at writing as some Mills & Boon novelists, but I have now given up my job as a medical secretary and have become a full-time novelist. My family think this is wonderful! So you see, I owe a very great deal to the Summer School. Everyone is so generous with help and advice and I have made some very good friends.''

To conclude this section I quote from comments on the School from two members from abroad. Mary Hamilton Moe writes: ''While the entire week is a rewarding experience for all at Swanwick, for those from other countries there is an *extra bonus* – that of befriending and sharing a common life with British writers from all parts of the U.K. and all walks of life.

''As an American green label I have indeed been

grateful for having been accepted for the 33rd and 34th Annual Summer Schools and rather imagine many compliments from the non-British are to be found in the *Comment Book*."

The other letter is from Helen Cameron, who comes from New Zealand. She has been to several Schools, including the last one, returning to New Zealand last October, but writes that she hopes to meet us at Swanwick again, if not this year then – some time. This is how she sums up her impressions: "I think the first impression one gets is the tremendous feeling of friendship. Many of us have met at Swanwick in previous years but even those who have never set eyes on one another before their arrival at The Hayes have become friends before the first evening is over.

"We are of all ages, from mid-twenties to early eighties. The majority of us have white skins, but those with black or brown ones are just as much a part of the happy family as the rest. People who write, whether they do it for a living or as a spare-time occupation, all need to be pretty good at talking too! Wherever one went, during the intervals when we were not attending lectures or discussions, walking through the garden to the little wood at the bottom with its pond, or sitting on the verandah, one would invariably find someone else doing the same thing and would probably join forces and have a good chat. Yet, miraculously, if one really wanted to be alone, one always could be – out of doors, that is – inside it was not so easy. One was seldom out of earshot of a voice, or rather many voices.

"All this sounds rather as though I were describing a leisure holiday. Swanwick is certainly not that! Though it was remarkable how, in such a fully occupied life, one *could* find leisure moments if one wanted to. We had come to learn and, in some cases, to teach, but I am sure that all those who taught us (and how efficiently they did it) learned a great deal themselves from those they taught.

"One good thing about Swanwick is that, however good or bad a writer you are, you will always find others who are better or worse than you! If you are a person like me, with rather a number of publications to her name, you will be cheered (rather unkindly perhaps) by finding others who are not in print at all. If you are successful you will very likely find others who are more successful, and be made to feel humble. A good thing, occasionally, for all of us.

"To the writer who has heard of Swanwick from friends and fellow writers, but has not yet ventured there, I would say, 'For goodness sake, go. Get your name down quickly for next year. You have to book a long time ahead. Once you get to Swanwick you will want to go again and again, as I have done, for more years than I like to count.'"

12

The Work of the Committee

The Writers' Summer School is currently managed by a committee consisting of the Chairman, Vice-Chairman, Secretary, Treasurer and four other members. They have three main meetings during the year.

The first is held in November. After the Secretary's report on the previous year's School and the Treasurer's report and statement of accounts, the committee proceeds to discuss the following year's School. Arrangements for the judging of entries for the scholarships are made. Subjects for the main lectures are decided on and a list of possible lecturers is drawn up, various members of the committee being delegated to invite them to the School. Naturally, we cannot always be sure of securing the services of any particular speaker, so alternatives are listed.

Next, the committee considers what courses shall be run, and who might conduct them. Course leaders receive a reduction in their fees (a small enough reward for their work), but are normally members of the School, though in some cases we prevail upon lecturers to take a course for us.

The fees for the next year's School and the London Coach fare are then settled, the figures depending, of course, on the charges made by The Hayes and the coach company respectively. Excursions are also discussed, since it is necessary to book well in advance if we want to go, for instance, to the Crown Derby works.

One of the most important items at this meeting is the Suggestions Book, which is read through, with all

87

comments being carefully considered, and often acted upon.

By the time that the second main committee meeting is held in May, a great many things have happened. The committee hears how many members have been registered for the next School, including lecturers and their wives or husbands, and officials, and how many are on the waiting list. Details are also given of numbers of "first yearers", those from the priority list (of people who failed to get into the previous year's School), overseas members, and of males and females. A report is also given of the numbers booked on the London Coach and on the waiting list for it.

The names of lecturers and course leaders are announced and the Secretary presents a draft of the programme for the week. The Vice-Chairman then presents a suggested programme of talks, discussion groups, panels and the like, with the names of those involved and the venues at The Hayes where they will take place.

A final list of excursions is agreed, and arrangements are also made regarding such items as dancing, gramophone recitals, competitions, the Secretary being asked to contact those who will be asked to run such activities. The organisation of the Book Room and the obtaining of literature which will be available in the Reading Room are covered.

A list is drawn up of potential stewards and first-aid helpers whom the Secretary will ask to perform these functions. The committee tries to avoid asking the same people to bear the burden each year, but this is not always possible. The committee also considers who shall be asked to be in charge of the amplifying equipment, to run the Lift Up Your Hearts services, to be door steward and to place in the Chapel a card commemorating any members who have died since the last School.

The third main meeting is held at The Hayes on the Friday evening before the School begins, the committee arriving that afternoon as an advance party. Apart from a final report on the membership and the consideration of any cancellations, the committee reviews all the arrangements, including those for meeting the lecturers, who of course arrive at various times during the week.

The Hayes. Part of the dining-room.

Two other committee meetings are held. One, on the Tuesday evening at The Hayes, is in preparation for the Annual General Meeting, and the other, held on the evening after the A.G.M., usually has two items only on the agenda – who will be Host and Hostess to the Speakers (stationery for the new year cannot be printed until this is known) and the date of the next meeting.

In between meetings, all committee members have work to do, including approaches to potential lecturers, and occasionally matters come up which cannot be delayed until the next formal meeting and result in much telephoning and correspondence. But the main burden falls on three officials – the Secretary, the Treasurer and the Vice-Chairman. The last of these has to contact those who will be asked to give talks, lead discussion groups, etc., and since nowadays there are usually upwards of thirty such items on the programme, this job, which cannot be undertaken until the list of members is available, is very time-consuming.

However, laborious though it may be, it is nothing compared with the work-load of the Secretary and Treasurer. Both are involved in an enormous amount of correspondence – with The Hayes, members, speakers, the coach company, the arrangement of excursions, scholarship judges, and so on and so on. The registration of members is a mammoth task, and is followed by the allocation of rooms, with all the problems that it entails. Then there is a great deal of printing and duplicating to be done, which is the Secretary's responsibility, while the Treasurer is looking after the very considerable sums of money involved, and making sure that between booking time in February and the School in August it is earning good interest. The Secretary and Treasurer certainly earn their honoraria.

At the School itself, again the whole committee is active. On the Saturday morning, before the members arrive, they (and their spouses if they are present) are all rushing about, putting up notices, laying out leaflets and magazines in the Reading Room, erecting blackboards, checking that the stretcher is available, making last minute arrangements with Wally Milne, and undertaking a hundred and one other tasks – believe me, it is no rest cure! And then in the afternoon, the coaches and the cars roll up, and the magic begins once more.

During the week, the Chairman's main task is, of course, the chairing of all the lectures and the A.G.M., and the Vice-Chairman gives out notices and makes arrangements for any additional talks or discussion groups (and rings the bell to say that it is time to assemble in the Conference Hall), and the other committee members are involved in taking courses or giving talks or perhaps leading or chairing discussion groups. Once again, however, the daily big jobs are those of the Secretary and Treasurer. I often feel sorry for them – they have to spend so much time in the office, answering members' queries, dealing with problems, collecting excursion moneys, looking after lost property, preparing voting slips for the A.G.M., and generally ensuring that the School runs smoothly – but they seem to enjoy it!

Finally, I must mention the Host and Hostess to the Speakers. Although all the committee members do their best to make the lecturers and their wives or husbands or partners welcome, they cannot always be on hand, and it is important that these distinguished people, giving their services to the School without payment, should have a Host and Hostess permanently available to see that their stay at Swanwick is as comfortable and enjoyable as possible. That is one of the reasons why almost all our speakers are happy to be invited to make a return visit.

Roy Huse, West Sussex County Librarian and a lecturer at the 1982 School, wrote: "Having seen the level of organisation and the enthusiasm and dedication of the committee members, I now know why the School has been so consistently successful. Long may it continue."

Epilogue

What of the Future?

Anyone reading this book, who has not been to Swanwick, will think that I am blindly prejudiced in its favour. Of course I am. But, wanting to make sure that the School still retains the atmosphere which was so obvious in 1949, I invited any who wished to write and tell me what Swanwick has meant to them and what effect it has had on their writing. How I wish I could have included all the letters in this book! I was particularly pleased to have many very enthusiastic comments from several of those who were there for the first time in 1982. It would appear that the magic continues.

The School depends, of course, on good leadership. I have already referred to the fact that Marjorie Harris has felt compelled to give up the Secretaryship of the School after serving in that capacity for twenty-three years. In reply to a letter I sent to her congratulating her on the efficient manner in which she had served the School for so many years, she said: "Thank you for your kind remarks about running the School. I shall certainly miss it, but with this eye operation hanging over my head it would not be fair to take on the School for another year. It would be bad if the Secretary suddenly had to pop off for an eye operation. What would happen to the School if it was in the midst of registrations or the programme time? So I did think it was time to announce my withdrawal."

Happily, Marjorie has been able to be on the committee for the 1983 School, and we are very fortunate in having someone as efficient and willing and with such long experience of the School as Philippa Boland to take over as Secretary, while Joan Symons continues as our most capable Treasurer.

The Chairman in 1982 was Stanley Wilson. He asked me to quote from a letter he wrote to me: "My chairmanship of the School has been one of the few real highlights of my writing life. It was your efforts over the years that gave me this rare opportunity and I shall be eternally grateful to you for it." Unfortunately, Stanley felt that increasing deafness made it impossible for him to continue as Chairman.

Michael Legat is the Chairman for 1983, an office he has held previously for a four-year period. I feel that he has many of the excellent qualities of Cecil Hunt, both from a literary and a personal point of view. He has the same clear voice and ability to hold an apparently effortless control on all meetings. He has written a highly acclaimed book on author/publisher relationships, and has many professional qualifications in the literary and publishing world, including that of being a successful novelist. Above all, he has the same willingness to help aspiring authors as had Cecil Hunt.

As the years go by, the leaders of the School change, but I think we can say that those in command now are of the same high calibre as those who started the School (if I may be so immodest, since I was among them), and there is good reason to believe that if those presently at the helm cannot, for whatever reason, continue in the positions they now hold, the School will produce worthy successors. It will therefore not fail to pursue its onward course and fulfil its purpose.

Long may the Writers' Summer School flourish.

SUMMER SCHOOL OFFICERS
1949–1983

FOUNDER LIFE MEMBERS

John Boland	From 1961 to 1976 (deceased)
Nancy Martin	From 1961
Marjorie Harris	From 1977

Honorary Member

Philippa Boland   From 1978

Chairmen		*Secretaries*		*Treasurers*	
Cecil Hunt	1949–51	Nancy Martin	1949–50	Brian Sutton	1949
Garry Hogg	1952–55			Nancy Martin	1950
Alan Wykes	1956–57	Eileen Jackson	1951	Eileen Jackson	1951
John Boland	1958–60			Beth Hogg	1952–55
W. G. Smith	1961–63	Beth Hogg	1952–55	Nancy Martin	1956
Alan Wykes	1964			Leslie B. Salmon	1957–59
Alex Stuart	1965–67	Nancy Martin	1956–59	Tom Prideaux	1960
W. G. Smith	1968–69			Marjorie Harris	1961
Vivian Stuart	1970–72	Marjorie Harris	1960–82	Ronald Simmonds	1962–64
John Boland & Nancy Martin	1973–75			Maurice Symons	1965–69
		Philippa Boland	1983–	Ronald Simmonds	1970–72
Dianne Doubtfire	1976–77			Joan Symons	1973–
Michael Legat	1978–81				
Stanley Wilson	1982				
Michael Legat	1983–				

LECTURERS – 1949–1982

Aldiss, Brian W., 1963
Allen, Trevor, 1949
Anderson, Jean, 1980
Aronson, Theo, 1981
Ascoli, David, 1965
Ash, William, 1980
Atkinson, Alex, 1956

Bailey, Bernadine, 1970
Barry, Michael, 1952
Barstow, Stan, 1967
Bartlett, Michael, 1979
Bawden, Nina, 1976
Bayley, Phyllis, 1957
Beck, Alice Hooper, 1952
Benn, John, 1949
Bentley, Phyllis, 1952

Berg, Leila, 1968
Bianchi, Jacqui, 1981
Black, Dorothy, 1967
Blandford, Percy W., 1981
Blishen, Edward, 1969/79
Bloom, Ursula, 1958/70/73
Boardman, Tom, 1958
Boland, John, 1961
Bonham-Carter, Victor, 1970/79
Boothroyd, Basil, 1956/64
Bowden, Jean, 1979
Bowden, Sally, 1975
Braddon, Russell, 1961/66
Braine, John, 1977
Brand, Christiana, 1962
Bridge, Antony, 1979

Brittain, Vera, 1958
Britton, Ann, 1959
Brophy, John, 1949
Brown, Pamela, 1956
Brown, Spencer Curtis, 1952
Bruton, Eric, 1959
Bryant, Joan, 1971
Buckeridge, Anthony, 1955/66
Bull, Donald, 1960
Bull, Peter, 1982
Bullett, Gerald, 1952
Burchell, Mary, 1961
Burton, S. H., 1981

Campbell, Patrick, 1956

94

Campton, David, 1975
Carr, John Dickson, 1956/57
Carstairs, John Paddy,
   1955
Church, Richard, 1954
Clarke, Arthur C., 1953
Clarke, Windsor, 1969
Clewes, Dorothy, 1958
Clewes, Winston, 1954
Coleby, John, 1973
Coleridge, Arthur, 1956
Coleridge, Lady Georgina,
   1956/69
Collison, Robert, 1973
Connell, John, 1955
Cookson, Catherine, 1969
Cooper, Elsie M., 1951
Cooper, Lettice, 1960/67
Cooper, Dr. R. A., 1978
Coppard, A. E., 1949
Corley, Anthony, 1978
Cotterill, Laurence, 1968
Cowley, Patricia, 1980
Cox, Constance, 1967
Coysh, A. W., 1972
Creasey, John, 1965
Crisp, N. J., 1969
Croft Cooke, Rupert, 1951

Daly, Dorothy, 1955/62
Daniels, Vivian, 1966
Davies, John, 1956/72
Delderfield, R. F., 1958
Dickinson, Peter, 1966
Dicks, Terrance, 1973
Dobkin, Maureen, 1974
Drabble, Margaret, 1976
Driscoll, Dennis, 1961/70
Dudley, Ernest, 1950
Duke, Madelaine, 1969/81
Dunbar, Janet, 1973

Edelman, Maurice, 1963
Elliott, Desmond, 1962
Ewer, Monica, 1955
Ewer, W. N., 1959

Finch, Helen, 1970
Findlater, Carole, 1964
Fitt, Mary, 1953
Fitton, Alan, 1958
Forrester, Larry, 1961
Forsyth, James, 1972
Foyle, Christina, 1953

Frankau, Pamela, 1962

Gardner, Derek, 1961
Garland, Ailsa, 1975
Gellis, Roberta, 1980
George, Daniel, 1959
George, Margaret, 1980
Gerson, Noel Bertram, 1982
Gibbs, Evelyn, 1974
Gielgud, Val, 1959/70
Gilbert, Michael, 1959
Gillon, Diana & Meir, 1954
Gittens, John, 1970
Goff, Martyn, 1971
Gould, Sheila, 1973
Gould-Davies, Anthony
   John, 1980
Graham, Winston, 1966
Greene, Elaine, 1955
Greenfield, George, 1982
Groom, Arthur, 1957
Grose, Helena, 1949
Grosvenor, Peter, 1966
Gutsche, Thelma, 1971

Halward, Leslie, 1957
Hamilton, Alex, 1968
Hardwick, Michael &
   Molly, 1963
Harris, Harold, 1958/66/77
Harrison, Sheila, 1972/77
Harsent, David, 1978
Hartley, L. P., 1954
Hartnoll, Phyllis, 1966
Harwood-Smart, Felicity,
   1974
Hern, Anthony, 1965/82
Hill, Trevor, 1953
Hinde, Thomas, 1981
Hodgkin, Marni, 1973
Hogg, Garry, 1950
Holroyd, Sam, 1981
Holt, Victoria, 1966
Home, Evelyn, 1963
Home, William Douglas,
   1979
Hopkins, Kenneth, 1963
Hough, Richard, 1954
Howard, Mary, 1966
Hughes, Shirley, 1982
Hulke, Malcolm, 1971
Humphreys, Paul, 1960
Hunter, N. C., 1954
Huse, Roy J., 1982

Hutchings, F. G. B., 1953
Hyland, Jodi, 1954

Imison, Richard, 1968
Innes, Hammond, 1952
Iremonger, Lucille, 1951
Irwin, Margaret, 1950

James, P. D., 1976/79
Jarvis, Philip, 1970
Jenkins, Elizabeth, 1962/69/
   74
Jenkins, Martin, 1976/78
Jones, Olive, 1953/64

Kay, Ernest, 1963
Keating, H. R. F., 1972
Kester, Max, 1955
King, Philip, 1968

Lambert, J. W., 1968
Legat, Michael, 1964/72/76
Lewis, Maynah, 1982
Ley, Alice Chetwynd, 1975
Lindop, Audrey Erskine,
   1963/68/78
Lindsay, Kenneth, 1949
Lovesey, Peter, 1980
Luscombe, William, 1956/
   67/73
Lusty, Robert, 1969

Machin, David, 1982
Mackinlay, Leila, 1960
Malin, Marilyn, 1977
Martin, Nancy, 1976
Mason, Michael, 1964
Mather, Berkely, 1959
Maxwell, Bennett, 1964
McCutchan, Philip, 1967
McDavid, Jack, 1976
McDougall, Brenda, 1971
McGregor-Hastie, Roy,
   1960
McLaughlin, John, 1978
Menzies, Victor, 1957
Meynell, Laurence, 1953
Minney, R. J., 1964
Moore, John, 1949
Morris, Brian, 1981

Nairne, Campbell, 1952
Neill, Robert, 1967
Newman, Andrea, 1977

Newman, Bernard, 1951
Newman, H. Edward, 1951
Nockles, Maurice, 1974
Nolan, Frederick, 1978
Norrie, Ian, 1965

Osband, Gillian, 1978
Osborne, Edgar, 1949

Paice, Eric, 1982
Pain, Gwen, 1952
Parker, Anthony, 1955
Parker, Charles, 1974,
Peach, L. du Garde, 1950
Pearson, Diane, 1977/81
Pitman, Robert, 1961
Pitt, Barrie, 1964
Plaidy, Jean, 1959
Pollinger, Gerald, 1958
Pottersman, Arthur, 1965
Prior, Allan, 1968/78
Pudney, John, 1955/61
Pughe, Cynthia, 1949

Quigley, Janet, 1954

Ramsey, Clark, 1960
Rayner, Claire, 1978
Ridley, Jasper, 1982
Ritchie, Dr. Carson, 1967
Roberts, David, 1962
Roberts, Nesta, 1956
Robins, Denise, 1965
Robinson, Oliver, 1957
Rose, David, 1977
Routledge, Carl, 1962
Rumbelow, Donald, 1973
Russell, Roy, 1974/75/80

Saville, Malcolm, 1951/71
Sawyer, Nancy & John 1979
Saxby, Lesley, 1968
Scannell, Vernon, 1974
Scott, Paul, 1959/65/67/73
Scott-Moncrieff, Joanna,
   1962
Settle, Alison, 1960
Sherriff, R. C., 1950/60
Shipway, George, 1972
Silkin, Jon, 1975
Silverstone, Trevor, 1969
Simon, Charles, 1963
Simpson, Keith, 1970
Singleton, Frank, 1953/62
Singleton, Jack, 1965
Sisson, Rosemary Anne,
   1972/76
Slaughter, Audrey, 1967
Smith, Frederick E., 1980
Smith, John, 1965/70/77
Smith, W. G., 1959
Stacey, Roy, 1976
Starr, Leonora, 1950
Steen, Marguerite, 1949
Stott, Mary, 1972
Streatfeild, Noel, 1949/61
Stringfellow, Olga, 1965
Strong, L. A. G., 1950/51
Stuart, Alex, 1960
Stuart, Vivian, 1977
Stubbs, Jean, 1974/79
Swinson, Arthur, 1964
Symons, Julian, 1958/68

Taylor, H. A., 1951
Thomson, A. A., 1951/62
Thomson, Christine
   Campbell, 1957

Thwaite, Ann, 1974
Tickell, Jerrard, 1964
Tilsley, Frank, 1955
Tilsley, Vincent, 1962
Tomkinson, Constance,
   1957
Townsend, John Rowe,
   1972
Trease, Geoffrey, 1950/70/
   80
Turberville, Ruby, 1976

Unstead, R. J., 1975
Uttley, Alison, 1951

Vallins, G. H., 1952
van Thal, Herbert, 1957
Vesey-Fitzgerald, Brian,
   1954
Voysey, Michael, 1958

Waddington, Patrick, 1971
Walker, Peter, 1975
Watkins, Pamela, 1981
White, Alan, 1971
White, Jon Manchip, 1978
Whitehouse, Joan, 1975
Whiting, Ronald, 1979
Willard, Barbara, 1981
Williams, Gladys, 1977
Williamson, Hugh Ross,
   1963
Wilson, Barbara Ker, 1959/
   60
Wykes, Alan, 1953/61

Young, B. A., 1957
Young, Kenneth, 1966